This Generation

Han Han

Edited and Translated by Allan H. Barr

First published in Great Britain by Simon & Schuster UK Ltd, 2012
A CBS COMPANY

1 3 5 7 9 10 8 6 4 2

Simon & Schuster UK Ltd
1st Floor
222 Gray's Inn Road
London WC1X 8HB

www.simonandschuster.co.uk

Simon & Schuster Australia, Sydney
Simon & Schuster India, New Delhi

Designed by Joy O'Meara

A CIP catalogue record for this book is available from the British Library

ISBN: 978-1-47111-430-4
Ebook ISBN: 978-1-47111-431-1

Printed and bound by CPI Group (UK) Ltd, Croydon, CR0 4YY

Contents

— Contents —

— Contents —

Foreword

Han Han, the author of the essays that follow, has assumed a variety of roles in his career to date: a professional race car driver, novelist, and occasional singer and magazine editor. He is also China's best-known personal blogger. Born in 1982, Han Han may owe part of his appeal to his poster-boy good looks, but what has most impressed his peers is how successfully he has gone his own way in life, presenting a skeptical, irreverent take on contemporary society that resonates strongly with them. Although the originality and profundity of his ideas are sometimes questioned, the importance of his role in shaping opinion in China cannot be so easily discounted, given the immense size of his readership.

After an early childhood spent in the rural outskirts of Shanghai, Han Han was admitted to an urban high school, where he chafed under the weight of an inflexible curriculum. In 1999 his first-place finish in a national essay contest suggested an alternative to the conventional path of examination preparation and university entry, and soon he made the decision to quit school altogether and pursue a vocation as a creative writer. By that time he had already completed his debut novel, *Triple Door*, and the book was published when he was just eighteen. A witty and knowing account of rivalry and romance among a group of Shanghai teenagers, it became an immediate sensation, and other bestsellers followed. In 2003 Han Han added car racing to his portfolio of activities, and since 2005, when he began to maintain a blog, his pungent commentaries on culture, society, and current affairs have won him countless fans.

As a blogger, Han Han has written several hundred posts; some have been deleted by the authorities (or "harmonized," as their author might put it) within an hour of first appearing online. More often, however, Han Han has played his cards so deftly as to stay just within the range of what is officially acceptable. The pieces I have selected for inclusion in this book are designed to illustrate a range of Han Han's concerns and give the reader a sense of many (though by no means all) of the targets of his caustic wit, which include China's educational system, officialdom, corruption, inequality, censorship, and nationalism. The core of this anthology is drawn from the collection *Qingchun* (Youth), published in Taipei in October 2010, but it also contains a sprinkling of both older and more recent pieces. After the title essay and a variety of early posts, Han Han's commentaries are excerpted more fully beginning in 2008, the year when he really hit his stride and his blog commanded a larger and larger audience in the run-up to the Beijing Olympics. The anthology closes with Han Han's controversial cluster of essays posted in the final days of 2011. Their moderation, disappointing to some, reflects a view Han Han expressed in a recent interview, where he compared political commentary in China to motor racing: "My first point is 'no push, no change,' but my second point is, if you push too hard, maybe your time will be slower. And maybe you push much too hard and crash." *

Analogy, like sarcasm, is one of Han Han's standard tools of trade. While these two elements tend to come across rather well in English, a third aspect of Han Han's style—wordplay—poses a more difficult challenge to the translator. In some situations I have been

---

* "Han on a minute," *The Economist: The World in 2012*, p. 72.

fortunate enough to find counterparts for the sly puns so character-
istic of Han Han's writing, but in other cases a satisfactory solution
has eluded me. So, while Han Han's distinctive voice can still be
heard within these pages, its more mischievous qualities are not always fully on display. More than enough survives, however, to convey to the reader both the cut and thrust of Han Han's arguments
and the scathing humor that accompanies them, features that mark
him as a notable presence on the Internet in China today.

Allan H. Barr

This Generation

This generation

A couple of days ago, at an event commemorating the tenth anniversary of the founding of the magazine _Buds_, I talked about the clichéd issue of the younger generation. My feeling is, it's a mistake to talk about this generation and that generation, but if you insist that such divisions exist, then yes, there are things I can say.

From what I can see, this generation is really quite traditional. If their divorce rate is on the high side, that's because so many people simply marry someone in the target age-group or marry for an apartment—they don't marry someone they love. When they reach the age of twenty-five, everyone feels under pressure to tie the knot. But this point simply suggests there's no essential difference between this generation and those who came before.

Society at large, however, gives this generation plenty of negative labels. They're "self-oriented," we're told, or they "don't care about politics." This is unfair. To be self-oriented is actually not a bad thing, and many expressions of this focus on the self are a direct consequence of the one-child policy. I don't think that problems resulting from the births of so many only children can be blamed on the youngsters who just happened to be born under that program.

As for charging them with not caring about politics, that's a ridiculous claim. In the current environment, politics isn't something one can't afford to care about. Those people in the past, they simply found themselves cared about *by* politics whether they liked it or not, and the roles they played were just that of small fry, hapless victims swept around in the political currents of the day. Being a victim is no decent topic of conversation, any more than being raped has a place in a proper range of sexual experiences. The era when one can care about politics has yet to arrive.

Meanwhile, so many dissatisfactions and discords of the age we live in—as well as so many of its successes and advances—really have nothing at all to do with this generation, but stem from actions taken by their seniors. China Central Television's loss of credibility, and with it the government's loss of credibility, have got nothing to do with them, either. This generation can find some scope for their talents only in the fields of sport and entertainment, and that's not going to make much impact on society at large. People born in the 1980s are now, at most, twenty-eight years old, and they exercise no real power to speak of, so the damage caused by abuses of power cannot be their fault. If you haven't wiped your ass properly, don't try to use the younger generation's baby hair as toilet paper.

As for the other labels—dissolute, promiscuous, confused, substance-abusing, vacuous, depressed, and so on and so forth—I agree that these are tendencies that began with the generation of people born in the 1970s. But I don't think these are so awful. Faith is a fine thing, no doubt, but what matters most is where faith leads us. If faith simply drives us into the ditch, then we'd do better to stay put on solid ground and watch the clouds go by.

On the other hand, we can happily note that this generation has initiated improvements in general standards of conduct: basic things like not littering, spitting, or cutting in line have been habits gradually established by those born after the Cultural Revolution.

It's our elders' glorious tradition that we have to thank for those vices and antisocial behaviors.

This generation certainly has its shortcomings, but I believe that's mainly a matter of individual limitations. Even if this generation has a multitude of faults, to talk about them at this point is wholly premature. That's because the mistakes that we can see at present are the work of other people entirely: this generation's mistakes have not yet begun, and this generation's crooks and jerks have yet to show their faces. I don't doubt there are plenty of fools among them, but that is true of all the generations that have ever lived.

Why do you cost more than me?

April 14, 2006

Today I heard about a traffic accident in which two people died in a single vehicle; the compensation paid out to their families, however, differed enormously: four hundred thousand yuan in one case and less than half that in the other. I've read many such stories about how victims' families get radically different payouts—for the sole reason that one is registered with the authorities as an urban resident and the other as a rural resident.

Of the laws that have emerged in China in recent years, many have been conceived with an eye to protecting the people's interests—like the new consumer tax, even if there are some humorous aspects to its provisions. From an early age I was told that it's essential to have urban registration, for that way it's much easier to get an education—or to make a living. The whole idea of residence registration strikes me as rather comical, and since my cultural level is not very high it's not clear to me why a household registration booklet has to stipulate that Person A can live in the city whereas Person B has to live in a village. From the vantage point of low-level diploma-holders like myself, this is simply bound to cause trouble in romance and marriage. Later on, I got involved in the culture industry and made a nice bundle by squeezing money out of city people, and now it's others who want to borrow money from me, so that they can purchase urban registration. For whether it's a matter of getting medical treatment, or finding work, or qualifying for benefits, or attracting girls who don't have urban residence but wish they did, or getting smashed to pieces in a car wreck or burned to a crisp by a bolt of lightning, you have a big advantage if you are classified as an urbanite. It may take a big investment to secure urban registration, but the dividends are generous.

Once, during a visit to the place where I grew up, one of the locals was run over—no, it wasn't me driving. The family was even more heartbroken than one would expect them to be, and eventually I found out why: The victim was just on the verge of getting approval for his urban registration application, so the timing could not have been worse.

After my early years in the village, my country-boy physical assets and athletic prowess won me admission to a good urban high school, but disadvantages in other areas led me eventually to drop out, which is why the only diploma I have is from middle school. Later, when I realized that you don't need a diploma to race cars, I drew on my experience as a youngster operating a two-wheel tractor to begin competitive driving. When I went back home, I would find that the fields where I used to steal watermelons had been sold off by the local township—leaders need saunas, after all, and chemical plants need land. I noticed how the houses where my little playmates once lived had been demolished by the township for a measly compensation of a few hundred yuan per square meter and an urban registration. In my village, everyone all of a sudden had become an urbanite and had the chance to be killed in a traffic accident.

For peasants, tax avoidance is tricky, since the land and the harvest are visible to all. Things are looking up a bit with the elimination of the agricultural tax*—although, of course, where I used to live it wouldn't make much difference even if they retained the agricultural tax, because hardly anyone tills the land anymore, since there's hardly any land left to till. How much money can you make, in any case, from a small plot of rice? Much more satisfying just to sell the land off. So let's mark out a development zone, bring in some cheap little factories and line them up along the river. The poisoning of fish and shrimp will be the principal and the ruining of the surrounding land will be our bottom line. Professional achievement and banqueting at public expense both require adequate funding, after all!

Our township's basic development trend is as follows:

Year 1: Sell off parcels of land in rotation.
Year 2: Enjoy the fruits of wealth creation.
Year 3: Full steam ahead toward urbanization.
Year 4: Drive an Audi on every occasion.
Year 5: Now sit back and admire the mutation.

Quite scientific, really. Take the creek outside my old home, for instance: It appears in seven different colors through the course of a week—just a quick look, and you can tell right away whether it's Monday or Friday. Our local plant life is increasingly distinctive, with stems free of leaves and branches unencumbered by fruit, so we see excellent prospects for the future growth of the bonsai industry. And it's surely just a matter of time before our native crayfish mutate into Australian lobsters.

Perhaps it's not surprising that different people fetch different prices—after all, there's lots of inequality in the world. Many people would like to create equality, given how superior some members of

---

* China's agricultural tax was abolished at the end of 2005, as part of an effort to reduce the financial burden on Chinese farmers.

society feel toward their fellow citizens, and the death of a lowlife and the death of a celebrity (assuming there's a distinction to be made between the two) will naturally have different impacts, but if the price of killing an urbanite is automatically much higher than the price of killing a rural dweller, this just shows that our system really is unsustainable. The registration system, at best, is a feature of a society in transition, and I hope it can be eliminated at the earliest opportunity, so that we have a system that looks good and sounds fair. If, on the basis of a piece of paper, people are classified into three, or six, or nine categories, how are we ever going to create a harmonious society? In a harmonious society, surely everyone costs the same.

Social regression, government extortion

May 13, 2007

New China News Agency, Hefei (Wang Yan reporting): Anhui Family Planning Commission recently announced that Anhui Province is currently developing concrete steps to curb the phenomenon of the rich and famous having more children than they are permitted.

The authorities in Anhui, we are told, will, within the framework of current laws, regulate excess births by wealthy and prominent people. A hotline will be set up that will facilitate the exposure of such individuals, and in serious cases the names of the offenders will be made public and sanctions will be imposed. A system of levying society-upbringing fees will be strictly implemented: Where a couple has given birth to a second child without authorization, these fees will be levied at a rate of three to four times the couple's combined annual salary; for every additional child born, upbringing fees will be levied at double the previous rate. In accordance with the new manage-

ment procedures, Anhui has collected six hundred thousand yuan in society-upbringing fees from the owner of a private enterprise who violated the current planned-birth policy.

I have some questions:

1. Planned birth may be national policy, but doesn't national policy need to have a foundation in law?
2. If Yao Ming has more children than he's allowed, will he be fined more than a billion yuan? Is there a legal basis for fines of this kind? What if one of these days some local government has the bright idea of announcing that parking violators will be slapped with a one-hundred-thousand-yuan fine?
3. How are the proceeds from this huge levy going to be divvied up? I sure hope the departments involved are not going to resort to fisticuffs to settle this.
4. Why is this fee called a "society-upbringing fee"? Are they really proposing that the child be raised by society? Do I take it that the parents need no longer concern themselves with this—that they can leave the kid on the doorstep of the governor of Anhui?
5. How exactly is society supposed to have nurtured us, in the first place?
6. If it's so important to alleviate population pressures in China, then the best thing is if rich people emigrate, for that way not only will they not have to pay fines, they will also be reducing the population by more than three units—the greatest possible contribution they can make to this country.
7. This new ruling does nothing to resolve China's most real and most pressing problem—that of the poor having large families. If they have no income, or negative income, then logically shouldn't the authorities be imposing a negative fine on negative income, in which case wouldn't the government, in effect, be paying the poor for having extra children?

I'll just have to wait and see whether some bright sparks can answer these questions. I have actually raised some of these issues before, never anticipating that local governments would handle these matters even more foolishly. When it comes right down to it, this is a policy rooted in an egalitarian ethos. Actually, although people may be put out when they see that the rich have bigger families than others, this does not generate any social problems or demographic pressure. For a big nation to try to shape its policies to pander to its less well-off shows that it is dominated by a petty, micro-management attitude. What really matters is enabling the poor to improve their lives, or at least providing them with some social guarantees and basic welfare. If you spend your whole day jealous of Mr. X and cursing Mrs. Y, and celebrate with your several daughters and one son when you see some rich guy get fined six hundred thousand yuan, after you finish rejoicing aren't you still just the same poor man you were before? None of the money that the government managed to extort is going to end up in your pocket. For all we know, the problems stemming from these exorbitant fines will be a lot more damaging than a few couples having an extra child.

You've got to wonder, too, what the Anhui boss-man was thinking. If the police had it in for him like this, he must have really dropped the ball on the bribery front. Bad job there, I'm afraid. The international community, not knowing any better, is going to think he's the only person in Anhui who has exceeded the birth limit.

China is now a very unfair society. It's normal, however, for social inequities to exist. A healthy society isn't necessarily fair, but it needs to be just.

Regarding my debt to society

May 14, 2007

In my previous post I raised the question of just how society is supposed to have raised us, because I hadn't quite worked this out, but plenty of readers have now supplied me with answers. I'm going to quote from a few responses.

"Han Han, how ignorant you are! How could you possibly imagine that society hasn't raised you? Do you think that the street outside your house was put there for free?"

I have to say that this comrade has extremely low expectations. He's the type of citizen our government most appreciates—one who's happy just so long as he doesn't have to pay to walk down the street. But better not dream of ever driving a car, for though there aren't many highways in China, the majority of the world's toll roads are here and even basic national roads will charge you, even though when you buy a car you pay a purchase tax, a value-added tax, a customs tax, a consumer tax, plus an annual road maintenance tax and car/boat usage tax, not to mention the local license fee. I just hope that the street outside your house doesn't get picked out by some boss or other for conversion to a motorway, or you'll end up having to cough up some dough as soon as you leave your house.

"Han Han, your ignorance amazes me. The education that you received, the house where you live, the store where you shop, the hotel where you stay, the hospital where you see a doctor—all these are things that the government has provided for you."

This comrade, I feel, has clearly confused welfare and commerce. So many of the things he mentioned are money-making enterprises. Free public education is still not genuinely free, and the other institutions deserve no further comment. I'm grateful, of course, to our government for building hospitals—it really set an international precedent there, didn't it?

"Han Han, you SB,* if you were in war-torn Africa, or in Iraq, you'd realize how much the government has done for you."

This friend's point is an interesting one. I like the way he used an English abbreviation when calling me "soldier-boy" and also that he reminded me about conditions on the battlefield. But, like our first respondent, he sets his sights too low. For him to compare a peaceful country like ours to one that's fighting a war—now, that's not very patriotic.

Just how society has nurtured us remains a topic to which I need to give some serious thought. I'm sure it must have given me some support, for when there was a fire in our house some years ago it was 119 that we called to bring in the fire brigade (calling 120 and fetching the paramedics would not have counted, since you pay through the nose for that). We need to be clear about the distinction between profit-making enterprises and social nurturing. Social welfare is making some progress, but since the country is far from wealthy, the government seems always intent on treating benefits as though they're a money-making opportunity. I have now paid over three million yuan in taxes to the government (in my profes-

---

* "SB" is an abbreviation for *shabi*, a derogatory expression similar in meaning to the English "dummy," but more vulgar. Han Han pretends to misunderstand the term.

sion, we do pay our taxes, and my real income is all post-tax), but I'm well aware that if someone in my situation becomes ill or old or handicapped, or if my income dries up through pirating or copyright infringements, or if one day for any reason I can't afford to pay for my next meal, the government and the welfare system as they currently exist are not going to help me, and all I can hope is that I don't get hauled off by city management officers.

Naturally I'm hoping that national welfare will constantly improve and the government will allocate more funds to it—that little pot of hot money from abroad, after all, is not going to have an impact on our economic marketplace. But no matter how rich our rich people get, a nation that views wealth with hostility, a nation where the population at large favors hanging the rich to rescue the poor, is bound to be backward and deprived.

Finally, I notice that it seems to have become the fashion recently to assume the air of some underprivileged individual from the grassroots. I'm wondering if I need to employ a translator for my blog—given that there are so many soldier-boys.

How radical and ridiculous I am

May 17, 2007

A few days ago I wrote a column for Xu Jinglei's online magazine. It was my idea, because I've been busy writing a novel lately and find it difficult to set aside time and energy to write a full-blown essay, so I thought it would be simpler just to answer some readers' questions. Sex-advice columns, in any case, are always entertaining, and they give you a chance to poke fun. Unfortunately, because no translation was provided for my remarks, many defenders of morality had great trouble understanding them. That just goes to show how much damage was done by the language-and-literature education they got in school.

In today's paper they are saying that I'm leading young people in the wrong direction, and they express the hope that the General Administration of Press and Publication will monitor or penalize me. This is all because of my answer to this question I was asked: "What's your view on early sexual activity among today's adolescents—how some students are premature in sampling forbidden fruit?"

What I said was: "I understand and give them my full support, but they need to take precautions."

They say my answer is not only radical but also ridiculous. But this happens to be my view, and it gets you nowhere to say I'm radical—that just shows how out of it you are. I doubt very much that people these days are so easily misled as to justify the claim that I'm leading them in the wrong direction. In the column I also said that, to my knowledge, there's nothing strange about an erect penis measuring eight inches—how come I haven't seen these experts tug on their own organ to make it that length? This shows they aren't completely out of their minds. But maybe some people just like to throw a veil of propriety over their own shabby behavior. In addition, the chief editor of *Education Today* claims that an overwhelming majority of educationalists disagree with me.

But that's just fine, for in my experience those so-called education experts are all too fond of sounding off about moral issues while they themselves behave quite unscrupulously. Whatever meets with their approval can't possibly be any good, just as it's unthinkable that any movie that passes the censors could be at all worth seeing.

Age eighteen is, in legal terms, when one becomes an adult. But often I hear people exclaim, "I didn't start dating till I was nineteen." And then everyone is surprised by such a late start. What's strange about the situation in China is that most parents won't allow their school-age children to date, and many are even opposed to their children dating when in college, but as soon as the kid graduates, the parents pray that all of a sudden someone perfect in every respect and—if possible, with an apartment of their own to boot—will drop out of heaven, and their child must marry them right away. Now, that's well thought out, isn't it?

There are actually no such things as "premature romance" or "eating forbidden fruit." At whatever age, so long as both parties are willing, any kind of attachment or sexual activity is an intrinsic human right that should not suffer any interference or obstruction. That's my view, radical and ridiculous though it may be.

Traditional Virtues

May 28, 2007

In my last essay I made the point that there are actually no such things as "premature romance" or "eating forbidden fruit"; that at whatever age, so long as both parties are willing, any kind of attachment or sexual activity is an intrinsic human right that should not suffer any interference or obstruction. To my mind, this is a remark that in the broader international context would be considered entirely normal and would not excite any controversy. But here a lot of people are criticizing me, telling me that once I have a daughter of my own I'll realize what a stupid thing I said. Some argue that it's a mistake to promote Western-style sexual liberation, for that will destroy China's tradition of a moral and ethical culture.

Actually, all I was doing was telling you what is your right. If you're convinced that this is not your right and that other people are entitled to interfere in your romance, then I'm not going to insist. I simply hadn't realized that it counts as Western-style sexual liberation if I say you can go to bed with the person you love. Or maybe it is just your daughter to whom you are denying this right? That's the way lots of men are: when womanizing, they're always hoping their partner will be young and uninhibited and ultra-liberated, but as they have their way with someone else's daughter they remain firmly committed to the idea that no one should ever put a finger on their own. This I understand.

The virtues that we celebrate here in China—modesty, sincerity, diligence, simplicity, helpfulness, warmth, unity—are, in fact, the qualities that we most lack. We're actually quite hopeless at these things. Just take sincerity—when does this nation ever have a social environment that encourages real sincerity? You can, if you like, give me a hundred positive examples of these qualities in action, but I can easily give you ten thousand examples of the opposite. The reason why we have so many historical anecdotes promoting these values is precisely because, if you look at the larger picture, they are so thin on the ground. We have to rely on this tradition to create a fake image that is peddled about for us to study and get our kicks from. The so-called traditional Chinese virtues are just things fantasized out of history—all the more so these days, when we have fantasized for so many years about these virtues that really have nothing to do with us. But these virtues are certainly appealing and, to put it politely, they represent the ideals that our people should work toward, given that we range from low-caliber to borderline-defective.

Of course, we Chinese always rate the Chinese people very highly. We should be content with that. After all, a full one-fifth of the world's population thinks we're wonderful. If you dare to differ, you're a traitor, and we'll spit on you until you drown in a sea of sputum.

And don't you forget—our land is vast, our resources are rich!

On flying the flag

June 2, 2007

Today I read in the news that one of our filtered keywords has died.* No evaluation of his successes and failures was provided. But I was reminded of when he was top dog in Shanghai during my middle school years and I used to hear his name every day.

It's only when the state's filtered keywords pass away, I realize now, that our nation will fly its flag at half-mast. No accident, however major, that affects ordinary people ever seems to prompt the lowering of the flag to half-mast. The only time I can really recall seeing a flag at half-mast was when the flag was raised at school one day and got snagged half-way up, but that was a case of the flag raised to half-mast rather than lowered. I notice that in capitalist countries (where, we know, people suffer wretchedly under conditions of cruel exploitation), whenever there is a major loss of life the government will lower the flag to half-mast to register its grief.

---

* This is a reference to Huang Ju (1938–2007), who was mayor of Shanghai in the 1990s and went on to become a member of the Politburo Standing Committee. Because he was an unpopular figure, Internet searches involving his name have often been blocked, in order to forestall further negative commentary.

Of course, you may argue that they're just putting on a show, but we Chinese can hardly claim to be averse to play-acting, can we? So I hope that one of these days China can put on a performance for its people. Of course, we follow rigorous scientific principles, so we need to decide in advance how many casualties will be needed to trigger this event, and in our country, this figure needs to be set very high—at least ten times what you'd find in other low-quality nations—partly to show that our half-mast has more significance than other people's half-masts, and partly because, given the current scale of our industrial accidents and traffic fatalities, if we set the figure too low, our flag would hardly ever make it up to the top of the post.

Because it has never flown the flag at half-mast for ordinary folk, our government may well find it difficult emotionally to come to terms with the idea. I have a typically Chinese solution to address the problem: If we replace regular flag posts with new ones twice as high, that would make everyone happy, for then a flag flown at half-mast would still be at its normal height. Another advantage is that this would provide enormous gratification for our people's pathetic national vanity—oops, national pride, I mean. Other countries' flags rise to the top of the pole in the time it takes to play their national anthem, but with our extra-tall flagpole and our lofty national stature, our national anthem will need to be played twice before our flag reaches the top.

Of course, I hope the day will never come when we need to lower the flag to half-mast in mourning for ordinary citizens, for that would mean a terrible disaster had happened—at the very least, the collision of two jumbo jets.

Let's do away with student essays

June 15, 2007

As a reasonably competent writer in school, I participated in quite a few essay competitions. Before each event I had first to brainwash myself and check to see what slogans were in fashion at the time. In the days when there was great concern about the "Seven Improper Behaviors," for instance, you would need to cook up a story related to this theme. If I told how somebody was about to spit and how I dashed over, stretched out a hand, and caught the gob of phlegm just before it hit the ground, and threw in some praise of our great country for good measure, I'd be sure of getting a high mark. Unfortunately, I only ever won second prize, because there was always somebody who succeeded in singing China's praises even more effusively than I did. Even today I still feel like saying to those first-prize winners, "I really scraped the bottom of the barrel with my essays—how did you manage to be even more shameless?"

In recent years a number of no-hopers in the university entrance examination have submitted essays that were awarded zero points. I've had a look at these essays, and what they all have in common is this—they truthfully express the author's opinion. But our educational system does not permit the truthful expression of opinion—what it tries to do is discourage you from having your own views, and then, using teaching materials that are decades old, tell you that *this* is right and *that* is wrong. If you don't agree, it's not as though you're taking your life in your hands—all that will happen is that you will be expelled or will get no points. Or maybe you will pick up a few—as long as you make an attempt to answer, the grader is not supposed to give you a zero. But the only real difference between the successful essay and the failed one is that you think this way and I think that: What's the logic in you getting full points and my getting none? Even if I haven't bought into the master narrative, I should at least qualify for a consolation prize, no? And for an essay—something that lacks an objective grading criterion—to be evaluated on the basis of the appraiser's personal tastes and incorporated into a university entrance exam that professes to be fair: This in itself is unfair.

Fortunately, though students care about the marks they get for their essays, they have little interest in the essay assignments. It's things written off as junk culture that enable them to salvage a few shreds of imagination and creativity.

It's fair to say that many people's experience of telling lies starts with writing essays, just as their limited experience of telling the truth starts with writing love letters. From an early age, model essays and essay-writing textbooks convey to students that the function of an essay is to eulogize and extol—to expose and censure, on the other hand, is considered negative and downbeat, dark and bleak. Some people may like to use Lu Xun as an example of how to get a point across,* but the role he plays in the school textbooks is eulogy and extolment too, with him as the lead vocalist. Praise and appreciation are good things, of course—who doesn't like praise

---

* Work by Lu Xun (1881–1936), an influential left-wing writer, has been regularly included in the Chinese school curriculum since 1949.

and appreciation? The problem is that the subjects we can praise and appreciate are dictated to us. You're not allowed to eulogize a girl's butt, for instance, or extol a hooker's technique. All kinds of restrictions force our essays into a straightjacket, until in the end everything we write is fake.

Naturally, loyalists of the old guard may well say that no matter the quality of the essay, this kind of writing does develop a student's ability to deploy language and create sentences, just as mathematics, though it has limited application after a certain point, fosters skill in logical analysis. Such people exemplify exactly the kind of blinkered and defective thinking that Chinese education fosters. They are simply underestimating their own intelligence. The ability to write develops hand in hand with skill in logical analysis: After you learn to read and accumulate some experience in reading, you are naturally capable of writing essays—if you can talk, you can write. Of course, some people can write better than others, and there's not much one can do about that. At the same time, the ability to analyze things logically is not something one can acquire or enhance just through working on a few math problems—that's just self-deception. Many scam artists capable of meticulous thought and impeccable logic have never had much education, whereas most people taken in by a scam will happily tell you the area of a shape in trigonometry. Our education system likes to give the impression that people have no natural talent and get everything from education. That way, after you leave school, you will naturally accept that human beings have no inherent rights—that rights are something only conferred by the government.

Education in other countries does not fixate on this same specialized concept of "writing essays," but I don't remember hearing that people in those places have trouble putting words together to form a coherent piece of writing. And conversely, in our case, although people here have been learning to write essays for many decades now, fewer and fewer seem to be capable of doing so.

Reading a lot is much more beneficial than writing a lot of

essays—which, in reality, just means studying a lot of model essays so that you can imitate the topic assigned. Essay assignments not only weaken your ability to write, but they subconsciously tell you that saying things you don't mean is normal and necessary, that it's the very secret of survival. That is the sole value to students of writing essays—writing essays alerts them early on to the reality that speaking the truth will only lead to trouble. But essays also have the effect of destroying their interest in literature.

Someone is bound to say that I am simply being contradictory, that I'm not capable of constructive suggestions—if everyone stops writing essays, then what on earth *will* they write? That's a typical example of the impoverished analytical ability you're left with after our education is through with you. It's simple—just don't write! Writing essays essentially is a hobby, a love, like gardening or fishing—it's not something you can force people to do. Naturally, there will be some who like it and some who don't. So let the ones who like to write essays write real essays, and let the ones who don't like to write essays write love letters, and let the ones whose love letters go unanswered write a journal, and let the ones who like to write fake, pretentious, empty-headed essays serve as our leaders— that way everyone will be happy.

Insults to China

August 11, 2007

It doesn't take much, it seems, to insult our nation. Often on our news broadcasts we see reports that in some country or other a shop sign or T-shirt or literary or art work is suspected of insulting China. There was a story the other day about a pet shop somewhere that incorporated a parody of Tiananmen Square in its signage and was forced to take the sign down after protests by our foreign ministry.

That certainly counts as high-level attention. If I were to poke fun at the White House or the Kremlin at a shop of mine, I'm sure I could live my whole life through and still be waiting for the United States or Russia to complain.

We Chinese people have very thin skins. We respond very poorly to any kind of unfavorable opinion, whether in the form of jokes, satire, or criticism. To us, this all counts as insults to China. In movies, we are always encountering problems of this kind. *Mission: Impossible*, I remember, was suspected of insulting China—on account of a shot of laundry drying on a balcony, apparently. For this to have become an issue gives you the feeling that hanging clothes out to dry is something that we Chinese never do—they've taken some custom common in India and accused us of it! Oh, dear—now I've insulted India.

Now it's *Pirates of the Caribbean* and *Mission: Impossible* 3 that have offended us. Every time there's a movie that is said to insult China, I make a point of watching the uncensored version, and more often than not I come away completely baffled. Far from evidence of insults to China, what I see instead are a lot of Americans making complete fools of themselves and foreigners being humiliated by the power of Chinese kung fu. And from the big movies these days, more and more people are aware that this is a nation that can't afford to make jokes. Apart from enthusing about the looks of the Oriental Pearl, it's best not to say anything else.* It's like with a little kid—if you crack a joke at their expense, they will make such a fuss that in the end nobody dares say anything funny. This is a completely different matter from respecting someone.

Maybe the problem is that I'm just not sensitive enough. Sensitivity and frailty are two major traits that we Chinese are expected to have, as a way of distinguishing ourselves from other nationalities. In this area I suffer from a real deficit: When someone tells me that there are various things they don't like about my native home, I seem never to get angry. All that happens is that I discuss the problems they raise one by one, identifying those that are genuinely widespread, those that are special cases, and those that are common throughout the world, and while I'm at it I mention a few other issues they have overlooked.

But when I mention problems in someone else's hometown, they often respond as though I have committed an act of gross indecency in front of their mother. If I ask, for instance, why the people there are so given to cursing others, they will answer with a torrent of abuse. I have never been able to understand this: So often, if

---

* The Oriental Pearl is a TV tower in the Pudong area of Shanghai, built in the 1990s. Its quirky aesthetics are not to everyone's taste.

we are born in a place, if we live in a place, it's not because we are in love with it, but because we had no choice—we weren't smart enough to avoid being born there. If you're not actually in love with it, the only explanation for your extreme response has got to be that you're just too wound-up, as though disrespect to your homeland is a personal insult. Even though these people privately have a whole heap of grievances against their homeland, their employer, and their school, they just can't endure for an outsider to scold them. "Even though I have no control over my own domain," they think, "if you criticize it then you're cursing me." When you see how they go for the jugular, you realize you have somehow damaged their faith in themselves.

But if I were to say to them, "Actually, I'm God. Sorry I made those unkind remarks about that homeland you love so much. I'm so touched by your determination to defend your country's honor at the cost of your life that I'm going to reward you with a chance to be reborn," I'm pretty sure that eighty percent of them would be off like a shot to be reborn in America, while the others would all be frantically trying to decide which country in Europe would make the best destination.

What's more, this kind of logic is highly elastic. So, if one day Europeans say something bad about Asians, don't expect the Japanese and the Koreans to be all up in arms—it will be we Chinese who react most intensely. And if one day extraterrestrials were to announce that we earthlings are fools, again it will be we Chinese who take this most to heart. If we encounter that kind of provocation, there's no doubt that we will organize—in best Chinese style— several hundred thousand people to assemble in the grasslands and form four gigantic words: "We are not idiots!" We'll do that in part, of course, to show those aliens what we're made of, but more importantly because this'll give us a chance to get into the *Guinness Book of World Records*.

The reason why we Chinese so often feel insulted is that we have so little self-respect. We like to think of ourselves as intimidating, sure enough: "People better not offend us! Our foreign ministry is going to take action if any little foreign shop takes liberties with our cultural icons! Just one impertinent sign is going to bring down the whole weight of Chinese disapproval on its head! Our film bureau can prohibit the import of any movies that we don't like!"

But do you really think this is the way to win people's respect? Actually, they're shaking their heads over how infantile we are. And we have no firm position on things, anyway. If a country compliments us, for example, then we're over the moon: "We're brothers, you and I! We just adore your splendid nation!" But if you indulge in any of that China-insulting, then we'd aim all our missiles at you if we could. And it doesn't take much for us to feel insulted—anything that's not praise sounds to us like disrespect.

Shut the door and have a look at our domestic discussion forums: When people talk about the Japanese or Koreans or Indians, you see lots of derogatory epithets, and in our chat rooms, shop signs, and news coverage, there's plenty of content that could be seen as insulting to Korea or America or Japan or India, and we regard the deliverers of these insults as patriotic heroes (of a minor sort, admittedly), and there's nothing to stop them carrying on like this, since we've never seen any sign of other countries' Internet users or media or foreign ministries registering protests and taking punitive action. So, our citizens have a long way to go before they qualify to be citizens of a great country—our citizens, in fact, still don't amount to being a "people" in the full sense of the word. Don't try to comfort yourself with the thought that these attitudes reflect cohesiveness and unity when dealing with the outside world. If the Americans were to say, "Chinese people are bastards," I have no doubt that we would be all ready to form a huge army to punish our assailants. But all the Americans would need to do is arrange for a few undercover agents to spread dissension in our ranks, saying things like "Shanghai people are bastards," "Beijing people are bastards," "Henan people are bastards," and "Guangzhou people are bastards," and I reckon that the whole army would be in complete tatters long before it got anywhere near the United States.

If and when the day comes that we are no longer always crying and wailing about how other people are insulting us, that'll be the time when there is no more risk of civil war in China.

Market day for patriots

April 20, 2008

> *In the run-up to the Beijing Olympics, after the Olympic torch relay was*
> *disrupted in Paris by supporters of Tibetan independence, protests were*
> *staged in and around a number of supermarkets in China operated by*
> *the French Carrefour chain, culminating in an effort to promote a mass*
> *boycott of Carrefour on May Day, a public holiday in China.*

On this issue, everyone is fully convinced of the justice of their cause: First of all, Carrefour's owners have done *this* and the French government has said *that*; and secondly, whatever it is they did or said, our goal is to make the international community aware of our attitude, demonstrate our strength, and force people to apologize.

To my way of thinking, apologizing is easy, but it's hard to change people's views about us, and after this business it will probably be all the more difficult.

Why does it have to be Carrefour that is targeted for protests? Well, actually it doesn't have to be—it could just as well be some other French company and we could just as well be asking: Why does it have to be so-and-so? But government propaganda always tends to seize on some representative example, and under its influence people at large are now perfectly capable of focusing on a "typical" case as well.

Boycotting Carrefour, I feel, is not patriotism, but a game for losers. An action that is truly patriotic requires you to put your money where your mouth is: When you are willing to shoulder an economic and personal cost for your beliefs this reflects a genuine commitment. But to kick up a fuss outside Carrefour is simply tacky. Another country humiliates you, and you give a supermarket a hard time. Some people boycott it, others deface it with slogans, or stage a demonstration, or just come to watch the excitement. Some pay for something small with a hundred yuan note, in the hope of making them run out of change, or there are people who lower the Chinese flag flying outside Carrefour and then take a picture to show that Carrefour is flying the flag at half-mast. I think these actions are all pathetic, especially the last one, which combines surliness with a craving for disorder. Patriotism can sometimes be a form of self-preservation, but sometimes it is a matter of the tone you set, and the tone we are setting shows we have no class.

Of course, you can reproach me and say, okay then, *you* do something more dramatic—lay siege to the French Embassy, or go to France to protest, or blow up an A380 Airbus. The thing is—why should I do these things? The idea would never occur to me. I just carry on doing my regular work, writing and car racing as best I can and improving year by year. In racing now, our level compares well with other Asian countries, and we can give the high-performing Japanese and Malaysian drivers a run for their money. Another few years, and I reckon we will have caught up with second-tier European teams, and I'm hoping that our best drivers will be able to rival Europe's top drivers . . . including Sébastien Loeb, the French World Rally Champion. Never mind whether or not we can achieve this goal—at least we are working in this direction. But what other people are doing is kicking up a fuss outside a supermarket—and if you don't join them, then you're a traitor and a sell-out!

34

All it takes for everyone to get so agitated is for foreigners to direct a few words of criticism or abuse our way. But with indignation comes complacency, complacency about how unified we are, complacency that "our country finally is strong, so some countries are starting to be afraid of us, and now they are scheming to undermine our territorial integrity." But I see no evidence that our people are demonstrating the kind of strength that would spread fear all around the world. You protest against Carrefour, putting the Chinese employees of Carrefour in a terrible position, and then more and more Chinese gather round, and a few disruptive Chinese smash a few things up, and then a troop of Chinese riot police is mobilized, and the Chinese media is lapping it all up—and I'm sure from start to finish not a single French person has been involved.

Those who support us and compliment us, we feel, are our friends, and those who oppose us and belittle us are our enemies. This is a childish attitude that reflects far too much concern about matters of face.

Why is our national self-respect so fragile and superficial? Somebody says you are unruly, so you curse him and wish you could beat him up, and then you say, "No, we're not unruly!" That's a bit like if Xiaoming says you're an idiot, so you go wave a card in the face of Xiaoming's girlfriend's little brother's dog which reads "I'm not an idiot."* Xiaoming will get to hear about this, sure enough, but he'll still think you're an idiot, even if you feel wronged and are convinced that Xiaoming is more stupid than you.

What makes me uncomfortable now is that there is simply no debate—you just have to show your colors: Are you going to boycott or not? If you boycott, that shows you're a good sport, you're a Chinese, you stand with the right side; if you don't boycott, then you're a traitor; and if you don't show your colors, then you are a coward. But I'm sure that if the French government were to loosen

---

* Xiaoming is a common "John Doe" kind of name and does not refer to anyone in particular.

its restrictions on immigration from China to France, there would be plenty of takers.

The situation we're in now basically is this: Carrefour is an inflatable doll in the grip of a bunch of people with urges they need to relieve, for a life of confinement requires some kind of outlet—and one that costs nothing. As they abuse the doll, they keep asking it and asking its maker, "You see how strong I am? You see how much of a man I am?" And when they find that others are not interested in molesting the doll, they accuse them of impotence.

Just what will happen on May 1, we still don't know. But I really doubt that people are so fired up with indignation. I think it's more that so many years have passed since the last time people had the chance to congregate and stage a demonstration. It's fun and exciting, isn't it? And doing it under the shelter of patriotism is a very safe bet, right? If you really can't stand the insult, if you really believe that the current situation is equivalent to the invasion of Chinese territory in 1900 by the Eight-Nation Alliance, that we're facing a national emergency—a critical situation with enemies on all sides—and the solution is to protest outside a supermarket, then I respect your view and understand your feelings. But still the sense I'm left with is: You just love to go to the fair.

Q & A with Chinese nationalists

April 23, 2008

Here I want to respond to comments left by many young national-
ists. I don't know why this is, but patriots have a pronounced ten-
dency toward foul language and crude behavior. I have had to do a
good deal of filtering to ensure that this Q & A session comes across
simply as a dialogue between two points of view. If the questions
seem brief, that's because I have trimmed them substantially, elimi-
nating a lot of emotional coloring.

Q. When a foreigner comes over and gives you a slap in the
   face, you just take it lying down and don't fight back. Are
   you just trying to show how cool you are?
A. No foreigner has come over and given me a slap.

Q. Han Han, a foreigner rapes your mom, and you still won't
   put up a protest?
A. No foreigner has raped my mom.

Q. The motherland — that's your mother.
A. The motherland is the motherland, my mother is my mother.

Q. How can you possibly think you're doing the right thing for this land of yours?

A. I own no land, and neither do you.

Q. You're no Chinese. A real Chinese would boycott Carrefour.

A. I don't see anything in the constitution that says that. This is simply your strong-arm, low-grade patriotism at work.

Q. Patriotism is a virtue, a fine tradition; it comes with us when we are born.

A. If, given the chance to be born a second time, you chose to be born once more in this country, I agree that this would show true patriotism and excellent moral fiber.

Q. You don't even love your own mother — can you be considered human?

A. My mom's name is Zhou Qiaorong, and I love her very much. Through my own efforts I make sure that my family has all its basic needs covered. If you want to make sure that your country has its needs met, isn't your family a good place to start?

Q. You say that the owner of Carrefour may not actually have given money to the Dalai Lama, and we have not been able to prove that he has. But that doesn't stop us from boycotting French goods. Carrefour is just a rallying point — what we really need to do is to boycott everything connected with France, like Louis Vuitton, like Peugeot, like Citroën. . . . Support the 2008 Beijing Olympics, and let the strength and solidarity of the Chinese people make the world shudder!

A. The modern Olympic Games were the brainchild of a Frenchman — Pierre de Coubertin. So you can boycott them while you're at it.

Q. We must resolutely boycott Carrefour. Shockingly, you are
prepared to let foreign powers humiliate our great nation. If
everyone was as cowardly as you are, our country would have
been swallowed up long ago.

A. Oh yes, you're strong and brave, you're not afraid to die,
you're a martyr—because you're so daring as to refrain from
shopping at a supermarket, because you're so bold as to put
Carrefour ice cream on a shopping cart and let it lie there
melting while you go off without paying, because you're so
fearless as to stand by the exit to the supermarket and curse
the emerging shoppers as traitors, because you have the
gumption to burn the Dutch flag as a warning to France.

Q. The Carrefour in Hefei flew the Chinese flag at half-mast—
why aren't you angry about that?

A. I'm sure Carrefour wasn't responsible for that—they
wouldn't dare. The flagpole stands in the square outside
the supermarket there. This action is typical of some ruf-
fian patriots—they were the ones who lowered the flag and
then blamed the supermarket and spread the rumor so as to
provoke people and make as much uproar as possible. How
unscrupulous can you get? So many things like that have
happened in other such campaigns.

39

Q. At this moment where the population is united as one, you
pretend to be clear-headed, make sarcastic remarks, and
pour cold water over the righteous determination of patriotic
citizens—this runs exactly counter to the popular will. The
fact that you still manage to publish your views goes to show
there's just too much freedom of expression in China—they
should close down your webpage.

A. Half the time you're urging the government to relax its
controls on free expression, but now when you find that

some people oppose your views you hope the government will clamp down on your critics. The country's trying to move forward, but you're pressing it to move backwards. You should be careful when you engage in this kind of backtracking—what's bad for others is going to be bad for you.

Loving our country, saving our face

April 23, 2008

I want to start by saying that, having received my education in China, I have no particular faith, and I'm sure that's basically true of all of us. The good thing is, I do have some humanitarian ideals, and I have never felt that love of one's country has anything to do with one's ethical principles as a human being, nor do I think that just because you were born in a particular place it is incumbent on you to love it unconditionally—or otherwise you're totally depraved.

Nonetheless, I must say I am very fond of this country of ours, even to the point that I am never keen on foreign travel. Apart from competitions where I am obliged to show up, each year I regularly turn down a dozen or more opportunities to attend events in other countries. Nor have I ever had the idea of going for a holiday abroad, much less the notion of moving abroad permanently. I prefer to stay here. Naturally, my interest in Chinese girls has a lot to do with this—I can't imagine leaving them.

What I tell them is: Don't do any of that street-protesting stuff. If you really feel compelled to join a boycott, then just take a break from shopping. I say the same thing to my readers: Just tell yourselves you've been boycotting Louis Vuitton and Peugeot for de-cades now, so you've already done your duty.

Again I appeal to my readers: Don't take to the streets, don't march, don't rally, don't do anything dumb. Now is no time to risk your lives and spill your blood. Just let things settle down. Let's just focus on doing a good job of hosting the Olympics. The last thing we need is more disorder. You young people dressed in the Chinese flag—please don't let things get out of hand. Just follow the govern-ment's advice: Marches and rallies will get you nowhere—certainly not out of the country.

On the Internet, though, people are saying, "See! After this boy-cott of ours, the French have apologized to us. The French presi-dent has yielded to our pressure. This just shows how effective our patriotic protests have been. Once again, the Chinese people have proven their mettle."

All right, then—you've boosted your self-image, I can see. In fact, however, so much of the time our real sensation is that we don't get the respect we think we deserve. Whether you look at things from your personal point of view or from the national point of view, whether it's a matter of slanted news reports by foreign media, or interference with the passage of the Olympic torch, or support for Tibetan or Taiwanese independence, or insults to our people, when you really get down to it, what triggers our outrage is that we don't get respect, that our pride has been hurt.

We attach supreme importance to this bunch of torches, expect-ing them to receive the same VIP treatment here as they move along their route that they would get in the heavenly kingdom, but now suddenly we discover just how many critics we have, and realize that they are no more to be trusted than CCTV. Actually, of course, there have always been people critical of us; it's just that normally we never get to find out about them, because CCTV and the New China News Agency keep telling us that the people of the world are our friends. This time, though, they can't keep the facts hidden any longer, so we're all very shocked. This, actually, is a good thing, for it prompts the government to improve its performance and gradually it is making some progress in terms of how it handles the news. Ten years ago, we would simply never have had a clue that there were problems in Tibet and that the Olympic torch had been extinguished on its passage through Europe. There are lots of things like this that can no longer be hushed up, so they realize they may as well be more open—after all, we are capable of coping with a certain amount of bad news. If people insist on boycotting this and boycotting that, to the point that in the future foreigners keep their mouths shut whatever happens within these borders, then the biggest loser is going to be the expression of opinion here in China.

There have been occasions in the past—like the anti-Chinese movement in Indonesia or the bombing of our embassy in Belgrade—where actual human lives were lost, but our angry young patriots have never before unleashed so much energy as they have in reaction to the recent provocations, even though our only real grievance is that we have been the target of some unfair commentary. We have more money now, of course, and so we naturally think more highly of ourselves and are more unwilling to take criticism. Also, the embassy bombing was a matter for the government to handle and the deaths that ensued were a matter for the victims' families, but this time round what the foreigners said and did was an attack on every Chinese person, and that's going way too far. When you extinguished the torch, you trampled on my dignity! Way off there in France, you managed to bully me, so from way off here in China I'm going to have you know—you can't get away with that!

If a CNN anchor were to bring a hand grenade into China and quietly pull out the pin and blow up a few people, I'm sure that would provoke much less indignation and much less boycotting and much less strident demands for an apology than if he were to say something derogatory about the Chinese people. We can be completely indifferent to the sufferings of so many of our fellow citizens here in China, but we are hypersensitive to criticism by foreigners, and this is all because we are so self-conscious about our image. All

43

those deaths and injuries, embezzlements and crooked deals here in China—they don't affect our self-image one bit, but those jolts we get from abroad do terrible damage to our big-nation psyche, that mighty aura we like to imagine we project. In an age of peace, love for one's country is nothing more than love for one's own opinion of oneself.

Patriots, please don't try to equate this conflict with the incursion by Anglo-French forces in 1860 or the invasion of China by the Eight-Nation Alliance in 1900 or the occupation by Japan in the last century. If you really think this is an issue of the same magnitude, your reaction suggests you must really be intimidated by the enemy! If you're so convinced that we've lost face, then go and win some face back for us, but just be careful you don't end up losing even more face.

I personally don't feel we have lost face at all. I think that here in China, whether it's a matter of our government or of private individuals, we are just as prone to criticize other countries, and to me it's no big deal if they criticize us and we criticize them, for it's not as though they've launched an armed invasion—all that's happened is that one side suddenly can't afford to get involved. It seems to me that if some other nation was in charge of the passing of the Olympic torch, then, with the exception of our country, where it would definitely pass off without incident, it would be bound to run into protests of one kind or another in other countries—perhaps even more. Along the torch relay course, whether or not the protests are based on the facts or not, whether they amount to insults or not, ultimately all they amount to is the expression of opinion, and we need to be capable of accepting different opinions, even those that distort the facts and are ill-intentioned. We can't go on over-reacting as though we have never met someone who disagreed with us, for that is just too embarrassing.

As our country gets stronger and continues to open up, we are bound to be exposed to many more things that we may find unpalatable, both domestic and foreign, and in the future when we look back we'll only feel ashamed of the way we once behaved. If you're so convinced that loving one's country is the quintessence of being human, then okay, go ahead and be a patriot, but don't be a Patriot missile. What we can't do is keep appealing for a more pluralistic society here in China, but then, as soon as we hear something negative and hurtful to our self-image, suddenly jump backwards several decades. Otherwise, watch out, or in the end . . . uh-oh!

Let's not get in a rage so easily

June 4, 2008

This year is a year with many disputes, and our people have accordingly got angry on numerous occasions. Of course, often we can't show anger about things that happen in China, so we never let the chance slip to get angry about things that happen abroad—for that costs us nothing.

When I heard what Sharon Stone said,* I too felt it was very callous, and I also felt that she had no understanding of the Buddhist concept of karma, because all I saw in the Chinese media were her

---

* On May 12, 2008, a severe earthquake struck Sichuan province, killing an estimated 68,000 people. At the Cannes Film Festival later that month, on May 25, Sharon Stone responded to a Hong Kong reporter's question about the earthquake in the following way: "You know, it was very interesting because at first I am not happy about the way the Chinese are treating the Tibetans, because I don't think anyone should be unkind to anyone else, and so I have been very concerned about how to think and what to do about that because I don't like that. Then I have been concerned about, oh, how shall we deal with the Olympics? Because they are not being nice to the Dalai Lama, who is a good friend of mine. And then this earthquake and all this stuff happened and I thought: 'Is that karma, when you're not nice that the bad things happen to you? And then I got a letter from the Tibetan Foundation that they want to go and be helpful. And that made me cry! And they asked me if I would write a quote about that and I said I would. And it was a big lesson to me, that sometimes you have to learn to put your head down and be of service even to people who are not nice to you. And that's a big lesson for me."

lines, "I guess that's karma" and "it was very interesting." I also saw a widely circulated video clip.

Only later did I read the full text of her remarks in the Hong Kong press and discover that if you look at her actual words we have no reason to be so angry. It's a bit like if the media asked you, "What do you think about the tsunami in Indonesia?" and you answer, "The Indonesians have been very mean to us, and so at the beginning I was very pleased, I thought this was karma. But later I saw the tragic effects of the tsunami, and my friends told me we need to do something, and that made me cry. I realized that my first reaction was completely inappropriate, and this has been a big lesson for me." And then the next day you find the media quote only your first two lines, that "I was very pleased" and "I thought this was karma." How would you like that, then?

This way of doing things is, in its own way, quite inhumane. Many media outlets in China quoted only those first two remarks, going out of their way to provoke the indignation of viewers and readers, including myself. We shouldn't attach so much importance to what she said, but we do, because among all the unhappy news reports we have heard recently this is the only one that allows us to vent openly and experience some release. Her exact words no longer seem to matter very much. After the earthquake we cared so much about human lives, saving everyone we could, never giving up even when all possibility of survival would seem to have passed, so why can't we go the extra mile for this foreigner who at least is capable of some self-reflection, instead of treating her as our enemy?

Humanitarianism shouldn't be directed solely at one's own countrymen. Naturally, if disaster strikes here, we should first rescue our own citizens, but a true humanitarian is concerned about all lives, even a dog's life. To be honest, when Japan and Indonesia suffered natural calamities in the past, the thought of karma also occurred to me, and I'm sure I'm not alone in that—when Hurricane Katrina hit the United States, for example, relish and satisfaction were obvious in the headlines covering the story in Chinese mainstream media. But I very quickly felt that I was wrong, that I shouldn't think that way. Apart from making a donation to the tsunami victims, however, I'm ashamed to say I didn't do anything else. Fortunately, these two countries didn't come out with any "Donor Rankings" and didn't take people to task for not contributing aid. But nonetheless I felt bad about not doing more. So when the earthquake struck Sichuan, I personally visited the disaster zone and did what I could to help. Of course, if I stay at home, people may think I am doing nothing, and if I go to the disaster zone, people may think I am simply making a nuisance of myself, but the fact is that during our eight days in Sichuan we did not make a nuisance of ourselves but helped out a little bit, and we never put on a show for the cameras. When I got back and at last had time to go online, I discovered that people who have time to go online every day directed a great deal of unwarranted abuse at volunteer aid workers like me. Even though this won't change what I do in the future, I have to say I find this disheartening.

In the aftermath of the Sichuan earthquake, the worst performance has been by those commentators who keep pointing fingers at others. One minute they want to blacklist so-and-so, the next minute they are cursing someone else's entire family, or exerting moral blackmail on some celebrity or other, or begging for money from some company, and they pretend this is all for a good cause, to benefit the people of the disaster zone. Most telling of all, they themselves are convinced of this.

The proposal to blacklist Sharon Stone, like the Carrefour incident awhile ago, makes me feel that we can't blame Chairman Mao for the Cultural Revolution—our people are just naturally drawn to mindless uproar. The good thing now is that there are some legal restraints on disturbing the peace, now there's a price to pay—even if it's just a hundred yuan, that's enough to scare away more than half these protestors.

As for Sharon Stone, if she'd made only the first half of her remarks, then clearly her head's not screwed on properly and she

49

fully deserves the roasting she's been given. But the fact is that she made the other remarks too, although you'll find virtually no trace of them in our domestic media. Of course, that's the way people like it: The entertainment news is all about celebrities putting on charity performances for our benefit, after all, and as soon as something like this happens, everybody can enjoy tearing someone to shreds in the name of some lofty principle. If Sharon Stone is a friend of the Dalai Lama, some people say, then that should automatically put her on the blacklist. But then, Jet Li is a friend of the Dalai Lama too. The Dalai Lama has a lot of friends, and some of them are friends of ours, and the most ideal thing—and what would be best for our country—is that the Dalai Lama becomes our friend, so that Tibet could be stable and at peace. But we get furious at the slightest provocation, wanting to blacklist this person, to boycott that business, to rail against such-and-such country's image—do we really think this shows how strong we are?

In the wake of the Sichuan tragedy, the great majority of us have shown generosity, charity, and concern, but after the media's willful manipulation of a faded film icon's comments we suddenly have become fierce and savage, with all our talk of blacklisting and dumping and excommunicating, particularly in this unusual period, when everyone is so overwrought because of the terrible loss of life.

If you browse through the chat room comments Chinese people posted in the past few years about the tsunami in Indonesia and the earthquake in Kobe, you'll find that the bulk of them talk about those events as karma—everywhere you see remarks like "Only six thousand dead, why not six hundred thousand?" Many of us still have a long way to go before we have a truly humanitarian attitude, to refrain from treating others in a way we ourselves would not appreciate being treated, as Confucius once put it. All these Chinese who relished foreign disasters and hailed them as karma and never got around to reflecting critically on their own attitudes—don't they compare poorly to Sharon Stone, who at least had the sense to realize she'd been wrong? We shouldn't be so harsh on others, and so indulgent to ourselves. I'm actually surprised that people from those other countries didn't make a point of collecting all the hostile comments from our Internet users and use them to stir up sentiment to oppose *us* and boycott *us*. I guess they are just not as cohesive a force as we are and are unable to come out with such a neat message.

A country needs friends, but our people seem to want only friends who can say nice things about us. We should avoid getting into a situation, however, where, when we really need friends, we find that we've boycotted them all and the only foreign friends we're left with are people more shady than we are. Sharon Stone, to be sure, speaks only for herself, and boycotting her doesn't mean we are boycotting the United States. But given the full text of her comments, I don't think she deserves to be condemned in such virulent terms. Our criticism of her is far more extreme than our criticism of the people behind the shoddily built schools and hospitals that collapsed in the earthquake. This demonstrates once again how selective we are in our tolerance of things: We can endure the suffering caused by natural disasters and the bitter fruit of man-made disasters, but what we cannot countenance is foreigners criticizing us. We're a nation that insists on not airing our dirty laundry and we shoulder our burden in the hope of winning other people's praise. When that praise is not forthcoming, the weight of our burden gets dumped on their heads.

What I hope most of all to see is that one day, when a foreigner says something insulting that hurts our feelings, we won't need to have everyone from the highest diplomat to the attendant in the laundromat make a statement about it, and the population at large won't have to all blow their tops off. As I see it, when others take you to task over some practical issue, all you can do is reason with them. If we can manage not to work ourselves into a fit of hysterics and avoid shitting our pants when somebody criticizes us, we'll be doing well.

Expressions of personal taste
strictly prohibited

June 21, 2008

The other day I remarked that I don't care for the writings of Ba Jin and Mao Dun. Bing Xin, I said, I find quite unreadable. Many literary critics, however, seem to think that a writer's overriding professional duty is to keep the joss sticks constantly burning in front of the idols. So they claim to be scandalized. "You have the gall to scold the great masters!" they gasp. "You insult them, you undermine them, and you pour dirty water on them!"

I find this totally bizarre. All I did was give expression to my personal tastes and reveal something about my reading habits. Things don't get much more routine than this—how can it be such a terrible crime? When I disparaged these authors' literary ability, these critics—if they are really so filled with righteous indignation—must surely take issue with my evaluation, in which case they ought to explain what is so good about Ba Jin's, Mao Dun's, and Bing Xin's work. If I disagree, that's fine—it just shows we have different aesthetic standards, and we can simply agree to disagree, and that would be perfectly normal. Or I wouldn't mind if they told me bluntly, "What an idiot you are to have such poor taste!" But what they say is this: "The masters are not for you to criticize. By doing that you're forgetting your origins. This is a moral failing that nails you to history's pillar of shame."

So, anyone who can't stomach Bing Xin's work is going to be nailed to history's pillar of shame. The critics seem to be anointing some pillar in their own home as "history's pillar of shame" and anybody they don't like will get their picture nailed to the pillar. If that's the case, they should have made the pillar a bit bigger, no? For, if you find little to like about the style and content of certain authors' work, this violates the moral code, damages the nation, and shows a complete lack of culture.

Actually, I have no trouble identifying authors who in my view are great masters. It's just that those you call great masters are not, in my eyes, great masters at all—I see them only as authors, or successful authors, and it's up to me whether or not I like their work. This has got absolutely nothing to do with a person's moral fiber. And even those people I hail as great masters—I'm perfectly entitled to say to them: "I'm not so keen on this particular aspect of your work." In the end it all comes down to a point that I've made before: The right to choose is a most basic right that you have and that I have, too. It's a right that everyone has. Of course, you may, if you choose, take the position that you do not have that right.

It's your right, after all, to renounce your own rights—isn't that a right that we love to exercise?

Appendix:
Highlights from the critics' commentaries

"Compared to the great masters, people like Han Han not only lack literary talent, but also literary training and personal cultivation, as well as a sense of mission and responsibility toward our literary heritage."

"We must never forget our origins, and even less should we curse our origins. This is a moral imperative; this is the moral compass that has guided the Chinese people for thousands of years. Whoever rejects our cultural heritage will end up nailed to history's pillar of shame."

"The masters are not to be casually doubted and sniped at. We are not qualified to do that."

"To belittle the value of the great masters has appalling consequences; it is extraordinarily wicked and damaging."

"To bad-mouth the universally accepted literary giants is an insult to a nation's literary dignity. To maintain respect for literary giants is an essential code of honor for a people and for a writer. We find it deeply regrettable that such erroneous and misleading opinions have been disseminated."

I'll do whatever it takes to
be an Olympics sponsor

July 17, 2008

Recently, as the opening of the Beijing Olympics gets even closer, I've seen reports that our government has begun suddenly to show concern for the protection of intellectual property rights. It's not the case that our government failed in the past to give adequate emphasis to intellectual property rights—it's that the government never thought they existed. It's very gratifying to hear that, with the Olympics, it's finally going to pay some attention.

I gather that, during the Games, you will not be allowed to upload to your blog photos or videos of Olympic events that you may have taken with your cell phone, because that would violate the Olympics' intellectual property rights; offenders will be fined. And within a set distance from the Olympic venues, there will be a prohibition on the display of advertisements by companies that are competitors to Olympic sponsors. This is a matter of national importance, and no objections will be tolerated. I hear, too, that commercials featuring Olympic athletes—the Chinese hurdler Liu Xiang included—will be banned from broadcast for close to a month, unless they are commercials for Olympic sponsors. In other words, because Cadillac sponsors Liu Xiang—of course, the money doesn't all go to him, a good deal of it goes to the Sports General Bureau— their advertisements will have to be banned, and for a whole month there will be a moratorium on commercials in which Olympic athletes appear.

I am deeply touched that our government is being so assiduous in protecting the intellectual property rights of the Olympics and its financial sponsors. I knew about its penchant for banning books, films, and Tang Wei,* but it hadn't occurred to me that it was quite capable of banning athletes' commercials as well.

It's fortunate that there's no motor-racing event in the Olympics, otherwise I'd be part of the national team and my books would be prohibited from being sold for a month, so that I wouldn't gain unfair monetary advantage from the Olympics. However, I have been looking forward to the protection of intellectual property rights for so many years, and it's enormously encouraging now to finally see light at the end of the tunnel, even if this light is not shining on everyone whose intellectual property rights deserve to be protected. But, taking a wider view, focusing on the national interest, I am not going to demand that the government protect my intellectual property rights, nor do I demand that the government clamp down on the hundred books spuriously attributed to me or the thousands of pirated copies of my work. Compared to the Olympics, what do my losses amount to? Compared to the financial sponsors, what do the taxes I pay amount to? But I do have a dream—to sponsor the Olympics.

If, by selling book rights and selling my car and selling my house and selling myself, I can qualify to be a minor sponsor for the Olym-

---

* Tang Wei's performance as female lead in Ang Lee's film *Lust, Caution* (2007), with its nude sex scenes, led to a media ban in China, imposed in March 2008 by the State Administration of Radio, Film, and Television.

pics, and if that helps the government finally realize that someone who writes books also has intellectual property rights, and if it then is willing to come to my aid by clamping down on piracy, then I will become the first (and only) writer in China to possess intellectual property rights.

Faking it

████████████████

August 14, 2008

These days everyone is talking about the Olympics pantomime: how young Lin Miaoke seemed to be singing a song, but actually the voice was that of seven-year-old Yang Peiyi. This fact was revealed in an interview with Chen Qigang, musical director of the opening ceremony.

The gist of Chen's remarks was: One of the girls had a better voice and the other had better looks. To protect our national image, we paired Lin Miaoke's looks with Yang Peiyi's voice.

Of course, putting it that way was not very appropriate and so provoked a great deal of consternation. Yang Peiyi, after all, does not look so horrific as to damage the national image, nor does Lin Miaoke sing so disastrously as to wreck our international standing. But I understand perfectly that in the context of the Beijing Olympics any interview is bound to emphasize the national interest, and intentionally or unintentionally it's easy to end up focusing on that, so, at worst, it was just a clumsy way of putting it. But what's more important—and what I personally admire—is that Chen Qigang was willing to explain what really happened. Even if the truth would eventually have come out, had Chen not been so candid it would be at least several months before people learned the truth. Lin Miaoke's family, for sure, would never have dreamed of talking about it, and Yang Peiyi's family would have kept quiet, at least for the time being, and the relevant government departments certainly wouldn't have spilled the beans. Besides, this is not such a big deal — it was just a bit of lip-synching, after all. There's no shortage of examples — is there? — of us cooking up some fake act, although we know we shouldn't. Everyone has built up a tolerance for these acts of deception, so don't act as though it's unacceptable just because it's a major event. Isn't it absolutely typical of us to play-act all the more, the bigger the event? And what Chen said simply illustrates that fact.

So I don't think it's at all reasonable to make a whipping boy out of Chen Qigang. Just because someone who tells the truth didn't explain things with the utmost delicacy, you dump on him all the bile that has been provoked by the bad habits that the state itself has cultivated — how does this make sense? In a country where things are being faked all over the place, in an opening ceremony that focuses on showmanship rather than art, to put on a pantomime is no big deal. Everyone happily accepted Lin Miaoke's appearance, just as they felt Yang Peiyi's voice was lovely, and there's nothing wrong with that. Lin Miaoke won acclaim, but Yang Peiyi did not, so for Chen Qigang to take the lead in making sure that Yang Peiyi gets the honor she deserves and for him to be so frank and honest — particularly at this moment, in this system we have — is something I can only applaud.

Sex + Soccer = Scandal?

August 29, 2008

Today I read a report that an executive officer of the China Soccer Association, when summing up the reasons for the poor showing of the Chinese national soccer team at the Beijing Olympics, directed criticism at one of the players, because during the tournament he rented a hotel room, checking in at 9:50pm and checking out at 10:20pm. Although his exercise routine was on the short side, it's very clear what he was up to.

This player is very unfortunate. For a start, it's clear to us all that the team's poor performance has very little to do with his workout in the hotel room. After all, it's not the case that if a player goes for a whole month without making love, he'll be ready to shoot as soon as he gets on the field.

The point that the official was trying to emphasize was the importance of discipline and obedience. But in sport, particularly a team sport, what determines the quality of the performance is how well the players play, and not that they refrain from checking into hotel rooms or growing their hair long or getting tattoos or wearing strange outfits. I'm not saying, of course, that if they were free to do all these things they would play any better.

In the Chinese soccer world, what we most lack are players with individual flair. But my hunch is that players with individual flair will never emerge under the current Soccer Association leadership, because the soccer system is just like the Chinese educational system—it places far too much emphasis on comprehensive development and collective mentality. Given the way the Chinese players pass the ball, I think they'd do better to hold on to it, for every time they take a step forward even my mother can tell who's going to pass to whom—never mind their opponents. So, beginning with the younger generation of players, they should all focus on dribbling and pass the ball only when there's no other option. Even if such a team gets lousy results, at least we might be able to remember their names.

Going back to the hotel room issue, it's actually very common for a player to check into a hotel room before a competition, and it's not reasonable to expect a player to refrain just because his ability is not that great. Similarly, in car-racing—the sport with which I'm familiar—taking a girl to a room is just a matter of course, no matter whether drivers are foreign or domestic or whether they're top competitors or also-rans. Many excellent foreign drivers are accustomed to taking a girl to bed the night before an event, believing this guarantees a safe run, so on the eve of a race I've seen drivers out in the street searching for a hooker even as late as three in the morning—and I'm sure the energy you use up in a car race is no less than that in a soccer match. Among good soccer and basketball players, there is no shortage of guys who like to live it up, so my position has always been: As long as you can perform at a high enough level on the field or on the court, then check into hotel rooms as you please; if you're not good enough at your sport, not taking a room won't make any difference.

In actual fact, the Olympic soccer team's performance was perfectly normal—that's just the level they can play at. What China needs is not to reform its players, but to reform its leaders. A player needs a sex life—those hundred thousand condoms supplied to the Olympic Village were not for the volunteers. Many foreigners came to Beijing for the Olympics, and although there are no openly advertised prostitutes in Beijing, a substantial number of the visitors—including the athletes—must have had sex during the seventeen days of the Olympics. This, after all, is one sport that all these sportsmen and sportswomen know how to pursue. So, we shouldn't think it's fine for foreign athletes to screw Chinese women, but then consider the screwing of Chinese women by Chinese athletes an explanation for their failures.

A week ago, a reporter asked what I thought this Olympics had given China. "A lot of mixed-race children," I replied.

Oh, man—what do we do now?

———————

September 15, 2008

In the second half of 2008, a scandal erupted in China owing to the widespread contamination of milk products and infant formula by melamine, a chemical product deliberately added to inflate protein content and increase profits. Tens of thousands of infants became sick as a result, and several died.

We boycott this country's products because it offended our
   dignity.
We boycott that country's products because it hurt our
   feelings.
We boycott the other country's products because it made us
   look bad.
We support Chinese products—but they just end up
   damaging our health.

Clothes must be new;
this is getting old

October 30, 2008

After the Wenchuan earthquake I said I had donated no money at all, when what I meant was that I would not make a donation to the Red Cross, because I was aware that they had very high administrative expenses. I did not spell this all out, for fear of being denounced as "making an inappropriate response at a key moment and negatively affecting the public's eagerness to donate." Later, my position was taken out of context and understood as "making zero contribution." No point, however, in making a big deal out of this.

Now we're going into the winter months, the time to donate warm clothes and bedding. I have a number of things—many given to me by others—that I have never used or just used once, so I was thinking I could just donate them. But suddenly we hear that used items will not be accepted—everything must be brand-new.

I find this very strange. I know, of course, that the government is keen to make a publicity coup out of everyone's eagerness to make donations, one that will exhibit our people's high moral qualities, high enlightenment, high solidarity, and high income. But when I arrive with a carload of clothes and bedding that are ninety-nine percent new, and you tell me you won't accept it, that I must buy new clothes to donate to the earthquake victims—well, to be quite honest, I just haven't reached that particular level of enlightenment.

For a start, these items are all good quality—definitely better than things bought for the express purpose of making a donation. On this point, I am selfish—for the price of five hundred yuan, say, I might buy a single pair of shoes for myself, but if it were to make a donation to a humanitarian cause, I would try to buy five pairs, so as to maximize the number of beneficiaries. When buying one pair for five hundred yuan, I would take into account the shoes' sportiness, weight, style, warmth, and brand, whereas if it's just to relieve an emergency I would only think about the shoes' warmth. Rather than donating a Louis Vuitton satchel to the disaster victims, it would be better to donate two hundred ordinary satchels—that is something everyone understands. And I'm confident that nobody's going to be so cheap as to donate rags to the relief effort—they may hand in items that have gone out of style, but not ones that are defective in quality. As long as things don't have patches, it seems to me, they should be eligible for donation.

Secondly, some places insist that items still carry the manufacturer's tags. But I don't understand what they need the tags for. Can it be they just want to sell the stuff off?

Thirdly, and most importantly, say I spend one thousand yuan on clothes and bedding to donate to the disaster victims, but because I don't know how to bargain I pay twice what they're really worth, so that the merchant makes at least a five hundred yuan profit from the sale—does it really make sense to have people spend their money like this? Surely this is not how we should be promoting domestic demand.

Finally, this is very demoralizing. If I put together a pile of almost brand-new clothes to donate, only to have them all rejected, what I'm *not* going to do is to turn around, meekly purchase new items, and drop *them* off instead. Of course, some people online may say, "On behalf of the disaster victims in Sichuan, I refuse these lousy clothes of yours," just as when making cash donations a while ago, some businesses or individuals contributed less than it was imagined they would, and some people online said, "On behalf of the people of Sichuan, I refuse your lousy money." I can tell you, the people's instinctive generosity is being steadily extinguished by these idiots. To start with, there may be a thousand people who stretch out a helping hand, but when they see how those who make somewhat smaller donations are humiliated by you so-called representatives, the numbers gradually are whittled down to eight hundred, five hundred, and then one hundred. You set a threshold figure for those last hundred people, and after further eliminations all that's left are fifty donors who have contributed the requisite amount—only then are you satisfied.

Of course, some may argue that the insistence on new clothes is out of fear that old clothes may carry germs. But that doesn't make much sense. Bank notes have passed through many more hands—when you accepted money before, why weren't you worried about hygiene? And even if old clothes have a few germs, couldn't you just disinfect them? Germs aren't so bad, anyway—if you think about the level of chemicals found these days in basic household supplies, you've got to suspect that new clothes and new bedding are injurious to your health.

If it's really so much trouble to donate clothes, then we might as well just donate money, but this takes us back to the question of where donations end up—of course the organizations sponsoring donations welcome cash most of all. Unfortunately, I still don't have a clue just how the hundreds of millions in cash donated last time were spent. No doubt everyone has good intentions, but in the face of the largest charitable donations ever in our history, we need to see a basic account sheet month by month.

Donating cash is nothing new, but the economic situation is not what it was. Although the economic crisis has passed me by, many friends and relatives have been adversely affected, and with responses to this appeal and responses to that, cash flow really becomes a problem. When the government organized the Beijing Olympics, it was very concerned about its image and loved all the pomp and ostentation, and now in demanding that people make donations it is equally committed to appearances and equally intent on extravagance. If I contribute a few thousand yuan, I may well be seen as making the country lose face and end up becoming the object of a lot of criticism, so I'm not going to take part in this autumn donation drive. I'd like to, of course, but I've been persuaded not to. I've encouraged my friends to participate, but many of them tell me they learned their lesson last time. They'll be scolded if they give too little, but if they give too much they'll run short at the end of the year, so they'd do better to just wait and see. Originally they were doing charitable works happily and in a relaxed way, but now they feel weighed down with such a heavy burden. Those people who peddled that message of "On behalf of the people of Sichuan, we reject your lousy money" have a lot to answer for.

To conclude, it's not that I refuse to spend money on new clothes, simply that I find this demand unreasonable. To demonstrate my sincerity, I'm not going to buy any more new clothes for myself, either, in the months ahead. Recently I've been watching the CCTV happy news, and I am happy to learn that our country has not been affected in the least by this year's turmoil in the financial markets. The people are happily going about their business, the nation is richer and stronger than ever—even to the point that it's about to come to America's rescue. So I feel I can confidently pass on to the government the task of seeing the earthquake victims through the winter. When it comes round to spring, in the name of the people of Sichuan I will present our all-powerful administration with a glass of milk and a couple of boiled eggs—put them together and it comes to a maximum score, 100 points.

We must boycott French products

December 10, 2008

Now it's our government that has called on people to boycott French products,* so as to demonstrate our anger and emulate members of the animal kingdom when they make themselves look bigger to overawe their adversary. But this time the incitement hasn't done the trick and popular response has been sluggish. As far as fashionably patriotic youth are concerned, they've already boycotted France once, and now to do it all over again just seems like old hat—it's not sufficiently cutting-edge, it fails to break new ground. Fashionably patriotic youth were waiting for their bosses' ideological apparatus to come out with a brand-new collection of songs, and now they find—damn it!—that all they're getting is just a greatest-hits anthology. Everyone's a bit tired of it all. So the government has no choice: like with the tax on fuel a while ago, it once again concocts public opinion, fabricating claims that eighty percent of Internet users support a boycott and ninety percent express indigna-

* In December 2008, there were renewed calls in China to boycott French products, this time as a protest against a meeting between the French president, Nicolas Sarkozy, and the Dalai Lama.

tion. What's different is that this time round I support a boycott of French products, for the following reasons:

1. We need a change in focus, one that will give us some fun. Our party newspaper tells us, "In terms of French politics, Sarkozy is really going through a rough period. The economy is in a slump, the unemployment rate is rising, popular support is falling, and so Sarkozy is making a play in terms of human rights and Tibet in the hope that this will distract attention."

It takes one to know one. The Chinese authorities likewise feel that they are really going through a rough period. The economy is in a slump, the unemployment rate is rising, popular support is falling, and so the authorities are making a play in terms of human rights and Tibet in the hope that this will distract attention.

The current economic situation certainly doesn't look good, and we're coming up to the Chinese New Year as well, so everyone needs a big hoopla like we had that time when we boycotted Carrefour, so that we can temporarily forget the pressure we're all under.

2. We can't afford French products. Because everyone's stocks are losing value, the economy is in retreat, energy is more heavily taxed, and so on and so forth. French products—which have never been cheap—now seem all the more to be purely luxury items. Seeing as we can't afford to buy them right now, we might as well earmark them for boycotting. That way, we can earn some brownie points for being patriotic, and bask in the glory of this exploit when the economy revives.

3. This way, we can serve our government's best interests. A vital issue: Our government was chosen long ago by our fathers and grandfathers, so it naturally represents us, too, and if it is correct, that means we are correct, and if it has face, then we have face. In an economic and political clash, if we win a victory then the gov-

ernment wins a victory, and that means we've won, but if by any chance things get out of hand, then we are to blame: It means that people who don't understand the true situation have been whipped up by a small bunch of agitators, provoking a narrow nationalist backlash, and our failing to understand the big picture will deal a setback to our diplomacy and cause damage to our economy. If we give the government an out, that beats the merit accrued by the construction of a seven-story pagoda.

4. This way, we can clamp down on corruption. We all know that the people who are now so happily boycotting French products are not in the habit of buying them. Some of them may well have their hands full just making ends meet, and others are no doubt unable to save any money from those fifty-cent rewards they get for posting comments online,* and I personally don't normally use any luxury goods from France, so boycotting French goods has no impact on our lives, but it has a huge effect on some officials and leaders who like to go abroad on "study tours." In duty-free stores around the world, they—or, more particularly, their wives—are the main force behind the consumption of French products. If we boycott French products, these people will be too embarrassed to hump those French luxury goods back to China. At the same time, since they are quite clueless about luxury goods from other places, for a time, at least, this will limit their spending and nip their decadence in the bud.

5. It can help my rally team. Although I'm changing teams next year, I'm still hoping that the Shanghai Volkswagen 333 team will win the 1600cc Class in the National Rally Championship, and its

---

* A reference to the arrangement whereby the Chinese authorities pay people to post comments on the Internet that are favorable to the government, paying them five *mao* (one *mao* is a tenth of a yuan) per post.

closest rival is Dongfeng Peugeot Citroën. If the boycott is a success and nobody buys Citroën cars, the Dongfeng Citroën team won't be able to keep going and my old team can win without even having to break a sweat. Likewise if you're a Ferrari fan, you can make Renault close up shop, and Renault, like Honda before, will have to withdraw from Formula 1 motor racing.

6. It can discourage officials from defecting. France has recently become the place where officials from Chinese study tours most like to abscond, and if Sino-French relations deteriorate further, inspection trips abroad will have to take France off the itinerary, and the possibility of tours of the European Union will also be reduced. Chinese officials will have to select other shopping and entertainment meccas for their study tours abroad, and all the preparations they have made over the years to defect to Europe will have gone for nothing.

7. This will reduce the financial cost of chasing skirt. Once the boycott really kicks in, you can say to girls who covet French luxury goods: "No, to uphold our country's interests, I am not going to buy you that."

In short, a boycott of French goods is on balance a very good thing. Boycotting Japanese products would be a different matter, for that would have an impact on our own creature comforts and most likely we'd end up saying one thing but doing something completely different. Boycotting French goods is much more feasible. All those hundreds of millions of peasants, workers, and underpaid employees of all descriptions have in their everyday actions for years now been quietly and unobtrusively boycotting French goods. Although I think it would be better timing if we waited to do the boycott until that day when ordinary people can actually afford to buy French products, nonetheless, at this time when our government has been insulted, what are we waiting for? We're already burning with indignation and our patriotic fervor will not abate. Now all we need is for those hotheads calling for a boycott of French products to be joined by the wives and mistresses of our officials and for them all to bring out the French products that line their homes and consign them to a public bonfire, and we'll be sure to come and cheer.

In praise of Feng Shunqiao

December 20, 2008

In the news this week:

> On December 6, the Hangzhou Intermediate People's Court
> found Feng Shunqiao, the former secretary-general of Zhejiang
> Province, guilty of taking bribes and sentenced him to a twelve-
> year prison term. The court ordered the confiscation of Feng's
> personal assets to the amount of one hundred thousand yuan
> and the recovery of illicit funds that he had accepted, totaling
> nearly eight hundred thousand yuan (US$116,827).
>
> The court ruled that during the period from 1993 to 2006,
> when Feng served as mayor of Shangyu, mayor of Shaoxing,
> and secretary of the Shaoxing Party Committee, he accepted
> three hundred fifty thousand yuan in bribes from a Mr. Wang,
> chairman of a Zhejiang company, in return for using his au-
> thority to seek advantages for the chairman and his company.
>
> In late 2002 there was a reshuffle of administrators in Shao-
> xing. A bureau chief in Shangyu named Zhang had his eye on
> a deputy mayor opening, even though he was a bit too close to

retirement age and had a poor reputation. Feng, then Shao-
xing's Party secretary, recommended Zhang on three occasions
to the local organization department, enabling him to be pro-
moted to the rank of deputy mayor. Thereafter, between 2003
and early 2005, Feng Shunqiao accepted, or received through
his wife, 446,500 yuan in cash or shopping cards from Zhang.

If, during the period from 1993 to 2006—thirteen years of economic reforms that offered very rich pickings to those in positions
of authority—Feng Shunqiao, a provincial secretary-general, mu-
nicipal party committee secretary and mayor in one of China's
wealthiest provinces, accepted only eight hundred thousand yuan
in bribes (a mere sixty thousand yuan a year!), and if you view that
against the backdrop nationwide, he has to count as having a very
clean pair of hands. Compared to many corrupt officials who have
amassed tens of millions in yuan through graft (hardly any of it ever
recovered) and are sentenced to life imprisonment (which probably
means release after twenty years), it looks like unlucky old Feng got
a bad deal. I hereby welcome him to resume his official career after
his release. If all our officials were as honest as he, if all of them
could restrict themselves to eight hundred thousand yuan in bribes
in a thirteen-year period, this would be a heaven-sent blessing for
common working folk.

Don't think I'm always having fun at other people's expense—
I'm being serious here.

Some points to note about whoring

January 4, 2009

What follows is excerpted from someone else's blog. I have not verified all the facts in the case, but I have personally heard of many similar situations.

> Today, at last, I can relax: My friend is finally able to go home to celebrate the Chinese New Year.
>
> A while ago this friend attended a meeting in Beijing. While there he went out one evening to a foot-washing joint, where he succumbed to temptation and joined the provider in bed. As luck would have it, the police arrived and hauled him off to public security. At first we thought it was no big deal, he pays the fine and that's it, but then he was sentenced to fifteen days' administrative detention, and later we heard he would be packed off for six months' re-education, and that alarmed us. If he got six months in the clink he'd lose his wife, and his job to boot. I'm not from Beijing and have no connections there, so I had to ask a friend to make inquiries. He told me it would cost one hundred fifty thousand yuan to get my friend out of

jail, and the man would still have to spend three months in the re-education center. The price seemed way too steep, and I wasn't sure it was necessary to go this route: Currently it was only fifteen days' detention, and maybe he'd be released after that. I visited him three times and learned about the awful living conditions (but that's not surprising—if people were happy there, it wouldn't have any deterrent effect). On my final visit I was told that my friend was certain to serve six months in the re-education center, and he begged me to get him out, whatever the cost.

I consulted various people, and a friend recommended a lawyer near the detention center. So I paid the lawyer a retainer of thirty thousand yuan, which would be returned if nothing could be done. This being the end of the year, the lawyer learned, everything was tight and the police were under a lot of pressure: If they didn't fulfill their quota this would affect their job evaluation, so nobody dared to approve releases. So he refunded me the thirty thousand yuan.

We simply had to wait till things reached the next stage. Sure enough, my friend was transferred to Dongzhuang correctional facility for six months' re-education. On the Wednesday—visitors' day—I went to deliver some supplies and saw a whole crowd of people in the reception room—men, young and old, hauled in for the same reason as my friend. As I left, he begged me to get him out as soon as possible, and I promised to do my best.

One day, when I was in Baotou on business, my friend called to say that a warden could get him out for fifty thousand yuan. I called the warden on my return to Beijing that Sunday. Let's meet to talk about it, he said, and asked me to bring him twenty thousand—the remainder would be settled later. We met in a coffee shop and he told me the plan: Every month the Beijing reformatory sends inmates to facilities in Handan or Tangshan in Hebei Province, and he could arrange

for my friend to be moved to Hebei and get him released from
there. This sounded very promising, so I gave him the twenty
thousand yuan. But two weeks later he called to say that the
year-end squeeze made things very tricky. If it were vital to
get the release, it would cost a total of one hundred thousand
yuan: another thirty thousand for him and fifty thousand for
the Hebei people. If I agreed, he could see that my friend was
moved to Handan the following day. I consulted my friend and
he agreed. The following day he was transferred to Handan,
along with one hundred sixty others.

This warden was a real moneygrubber, I felt: We'd agreed
on fifty thousand, and now the figure had suddenly shot up to
one hundred thousand—this was carrying things a bit too far. I
decided to consult a friend in Shijiazhuang. He was shocked to
hear about the situation, for according to him in Shijiazhuang
it's no big deal to consort with prostitutes: The worst that could
happen would be that you were fined five thousand yuan. But
he assured me he could get my friend out, though it would cost
him. I drove to Shijiazhuang, where he introduced me to someone who had connections with the provincial public security
department. This man said that calls had been made and that
Handan public security would facilitate the release.

That Monday my friend and I drove to Handan, where we
picked up a contact from public security and went together to
the Handan reformatory. But the chief refused to release his
prisoner under any circumstances, saying our paperwork was
incomplete: The application for release had to come directly
from his family, with a stamp from his home police station; a
hospital had to supply a medical certificate, and thirty thousand yuan in guarantor's deposit and over three thousand yuan
in stipend had to be provided. We would have to go back to
Shijiazhuang to attend to the paperwork and ask the friend's
wife to come to Handan.

Later we heard that this chief warden had actually been re-

lieved of his duties, and he remained in charge simply because his replacement had not yet arrived. This was his last chance to line his pockets, so he wasn't prepared to cut us any slack. Apparently his wife ran the reformatory store, which sold fake goods and was very expensive, and visitors were required to buy stuff there rather than bring things in from outside.

On Wednesday afternoon, we met the friend's wife at Handan airport, and the following morning picked up our contact and went to the reformatory. This time we had paperwork, a family member, and money, so everything went fairly smoothly and my friend was released. That afternoon we returned to Shijiazhuang, where my friend bought some clothes and had a shower. After dinner we took them to Shijiazhuang airport and I went straight on to Beijing.

84 Appendix: Expenses incurred in playing the Get Out of Jail Not-So-Free Card

1. Detention center expenses
   (arranging to see the prisoner)   5,000 yuan
2. Beijing correctional facility
   (tobacco for the warden)   2,500
3. Money to the warden   20,000
4. Expenses in Hebei (travel to and fro)   2,000
5. Payments to contacts
   (public security, warden, friend)   45,000
6. Medical certification   3,000
7. Entertainment in Shijiazhuang   5,000
8. Handan reformatory expenses (guarantee) 30,000
9. Six months' living expenses   3,200
   TOTAL   115,700 yuan

This blog post tells us a number of things:

1. This friend broke a law, and what he violated was the first article in the Constitution of the People's Republic of China, namely: If we say you've broken the law, you've broken the law.

2. In addition, this friend violated the first article in the "Public Security Management Law": to pay for sex with a prostitute in a business that has failed to pay its protection fee to Public Security or other government department will be sentenced to ten to fifteen days of detention and a fine of up to five thousand yuan; in less serious cases, detention may not exceed five days and the fine may not exceed five hundred yuan. One who pays for sex with a prostitute in an unauthorized sex business within half a mile of a sex business operating in coordination with a government agency will be punished with one month of reform through labor, and the unauthorized sex business is to be punished in accordance with procedures governing businesses that violate the "People's Republic of China Law on Unacceptable Competition." To pay for sex with a prostitute within twenty miles of Tiananmen will be punished with three months' reform through labor; sex with a prostitute at the end of the year when the relevant departments have yet to fulfill their quota will be punished with six months' reform through labor.

3. This friend really messed up. For 120,000 yuan, he could have 2,400 happy-ending massages in a "salon," or 1,200 dates with a streetwalker, or 800 sessions with a "hair stylist," or 240 full-services in a spa, or 150 deluxe saunas in a big city, or 120 college students selling it on the side, or 100 foreign babes, or 50 wannabe models, or 12 starlets, or 2.5 not-quite-prime-time anchor women. . . . When you think of the bill this man racked up, no wonder they say that women dread wedding the wrong bod and men dread bedding the wrong broad.

4. You need to be careful about doing stuff at the end of the year. What's normally legal becomes illegal then because the police have a quota to fill.

5. You need to be careful, too, about whoring in Beijing. If you fancy yourself a metrosexual, it's best to hang out in a city that's both metro and sexual. Other metropolitan areas do a better job of combining those two qualities.

6. If prostitution were ever legalized, it would be impossible to collect protection money, connection money, assistance money, and getting-out-of-jail money. So prostitution cannot be legalized; the only places it is legal are those that have paid the government protection money.

7. Some people are under the impression that fifteen days' detention is all you get for sleeping with a prostitute, but it's possible to end up with six months' re-education. If you're engaged in a threesome when they catch you, I'm told you may be charged with sponsoring an orgy and sentenced to five years. Friends with a taste for this kind of entertainment would be wise to select the venue with care.

8. Some innocent souls may say, "Let's treat all cases the same way and hand out a six-month sentence to everyone who's had sex with prostitutes." But be sure to whisper that, for if God should ever hear your prayer, when you wake up the next day you'll find that the vast majority of male authors, businessmen, singers, actors, athletes, directors, and officials are out of circulation—and that includes prison governors and wardens of correctional facilities. Of the eighty million Communist Party members there will be only 20,080,000 left, and of those, all but 80,000 will be women. If you turn on the TV there will be no programs and if you turn on the computer there will be no news updates, and practically all the men on the Forbes list of millionaires will have disappeared as well. Worst of all, you won't be able to find your dad. Perhaps some male readers will ask: Well, what

about you—are we going to see *you*? But you guys will be nowhere to be seen, so how will you be able to ask me?

9. You shouldn't laugh at this poor fellow's misfortunes. Maybe you won't be arrested for consorting with prostitutes, but there's always a chance that one day you'll be the one who's desperate to get bailed out.

No fire without smoke:
business as usual for
China Central Television

February 11, 2009

Beijing Public Security has now established, I'm relieved to hear, that the fire at the CCTV headquarters was not some mysterious case of spontaneous combustion, nor was it accidentally sparked by neighborhood residents setting off firecrackers or by part-time workers smoking tobacco, but was caused by CCTV itself fooling around with celebratory pyrotechnics — it set fire to itself, in other words.* The only upsetting thing is that fireman Zhang Jianyong gave his life fighting the flames, otherwise the whole thing would be pure comedy.

Later, CCTV issued an apology, blaming the fire on a certain office manager who, acting without authorization from his superi-

---

* On the evening of February 9, 2009, a blaze started by fireworks gutted the nearly finished north wing of the China Central Television headquarters on Chang'an Avenue in Beijing, which was designed to house a luxury hotel, TV studio, and data processing center.

ors, set off fireworks in violation of the rules. Thus was unveiled the most firework-loving office manager in all of human history: The computer-controlled release of a million-yuan's worth of fireworks and its filming by multiple video cameras were all the work of a single man. If it was not authorized by his superiors, then I guess he must have done it all at his own expense, unless at CCTV an office manager doesn't need approval to set off a million-yuan's worth of fireworks, this being such a minor expenditure.

Neither of these explanations holds water, of course: It's obvious that upper-level administrators are desperate to pin all responsibility on this office manager. "Hey, brother," they say, "just go off to jail like a good fellow. Rest at ease: We'll support your parents and provide for your children—and we'll give your wife our attention, too."

The fireworks display was clearly intended for screening in some future TV production, as a sequence in a feature about the new CCTV headquarters, or for use after that evening's broadcast of the Lantern Festival Gala, when they could wow viewers with the awesome sight of fireworks illuminating the famous "Underpants"—the main building in the complex that looks so much like a pair of boxer shorts. It's too bad that this footage is now all reduced to classified material. I can just picture how the cameramen filming the fireworks would have picked up their walkie-talkies and asked their supervisor, "Director, director, was this planned?"

I find to my surprise that everyone I know, though sorry about the fireman's death, is thrilled by the burning down of the CCTV building. I personally am doing my utmost to suppress my darker impulses and to respond to the fire with appropriate concern, but I have to admit that I too am relishing CCTV's misfortune. Of course, others may well be sorely grieved by this event, in which case I have to accept that my social circle is a mean-spirited little clique. So let me go ahead and reveal my vulgar, mean-spirited position.

First of all, as the saying goes, the reckless court their own destruction. It is a historical law, after all, that if you play with fire you're going to get burned, although we normally think of that as a very drawn-out process—it's unusual to find a case like this where playing with fire can have such immediate repercussions. As a media outlet, CCTV basically has no media ethics. In most countries, for a television station to do things the way CCTV does would be quite illegal. Here, on the other hand, it is not only legal but it is the very symbol of legality. Over the years, in just how many instances has CCTV been responsible for distorting the facts, confusing matters, debasing culture, twisting the evidence, engaging in deception, colluding in wrongdoing, and glossing over problems? Well, it's just a question—if you say it's never done those things, that must be true, I suppose—the media resources are all under your control, after all.

Logically, when the state suffers such a huge loss, ordinary people should be very upset, because the building was built with taxpayer money. But these days everyone takes a broader view. With all the taxpayer money that is squandered on official banqueting and entertainment, putting up a building not once but twice is no big deal. People tend to think of CCTV as a real ass-kicker, and CCTV likes to think of itself that way too, but when the fire burns its own ass, then it doesn't feel so good anymore. CCTV is a semi-monopoly, and when a semi-monopoly can think so highly of itself, then one can imagine how proud of itself a monopoly organization is. They're top dog, anyway, and you crummy peons are no more than fleas in the top dog's coat. Give me any more hassle, and that little heap of dog shit is your future.

Therefore, CCTV should engage in some self-reflection. Oh, sorry, I forgot—it never needs to do that.

With the development of society and the increasing sophistication of public opinion, we can no longer describe CCTV's credibility as zero—it has already moved into negative territory. In other words, our inclination is to interpret CCTV's news as telling us the opposite of what it claims to be saying. Of course we understand that CCTV, as a national television station and a mouthpiece for the Communist Party, naturally is not free to do whatever it likes, but still, it is always possible to do something reasonably well—reports produced on demand don't have to be quite as clunky as they are, for that leads to the worst possible outcome. When a media outlet loses all its credibility and not only is not closed down but actually carries on being the state's primary source of publicity, then one has to say that the state itself has lost its credibility.

The unfortunate thing is that in its handling of this fire, CCTV made the exact same mistake it always does. Apart from the huge forest fire in Heilongjiang in 1987, this has to be the fire that has caused the greatest financial losses since the founding of the People's Republic: No matter what, it has got to be a major news item. But it has been downplayed so vigorously by CCTV, you might have thought it was as inconsequential as a fire that destroys just your home or mine. If the BBC headquarters burned down because of fireworks, or even if Hunan Satellite TV headquarters burned down, CCTV would definitely report this most enthusiastically. Not only would there be rolling coverage, but I bet the director would be so overjoyed he would roll around on the ground in delight, taking rolling coverage to a whole new level. But such a big event—one that made headline news and warranted live coverage around the world—actually went unheralded on a national television station, "harmonized" to the point of total effacement. That is the current state of news reporting in our country: All the news we see has undergone a process of selection and deletion, and everything depends on the needs of the screenplay and the requirements of the director.

The issue raised by this fire is not whether fireworks should or should not be banned. That is a trivial matter. After all, this is just a little climax in CCTV's long career of burning itself. The issue we should be thinking about is: Should CCTV be banned? And the government needs to reflect on another issue, and that is: CCTV, *People's Daily*, *Enlightenment Daily*, the New China News Agency, and other such mouthpieces, under the current operating model, all have a negative impact on the government's image. What starts out as an actual event, after being reported by these media outlets and after a circular from the New China News Agency, ends up looking like something that's been cooked up. Something that is positive, after all their promotion of it, becomes something negative. And as young people grow up, the news items reported by the media simply become fodder for jokes. Over the last fifty years, so many social changes have occurred, but management of the propaganda apparatus and its methods of publicity are basically just what they were half a century ago, except that we now have ineffectual enhancements like the hacks who get paid a pittance to sing the government's praises. If the official media command no respect from the younger generation, who can be surprised?

Fifty years ago, people were easy to fool. In those days, if *People's Daily* had claimed that *Quotations from Chairman Mao* was circulating so widely in the United States as to trigger its collapse, ninety-eight percent of evening viewers would have been just as ready as CCTV itself to light fireworks and celebrate. But now we live in an age that believes in persuading people by moral example (or in deceiving people through moral browbeating). So I hope this fire will compel the authorities to give careful thought to this question: Do we really need the nightly news?

93

Like Jackie Chan,
guessing the majesties' wishes

April 21, 2009

"I'm not sure if it's good to have freedom or not," said Jackie Chan. "If you're too free, you're like the way Hong Kong is now—very chaotic. Taiwan is also chaotic. I'm gradually beginning to feel that we Chinese need to be controlled. If we're not being controlled, we'll just do what we want." *

Jackie Chan's remarks, though simple and casual, have a certain airtight logic to them—a difficult combination to achieve.

First of all, I cannot claim that Chinese people do not need to be controlled. We commonly have two ways of looking at the relationship between government and the people, the first in terms of control, as Jackie Chan has put it, and the second—a much less common formulation—in terms of the service industry. If we imagine things in terms of a restaurant, the government naturally

---

* On April 18, 2009, during a panel discussion at the Boao Forum for Asia, Chan made these remarks when pressed to take a stand against media censorship in China.

wants to be the owner and not the waiter, because while the waiter can charge only what's acceptable by professional norms, the owner can dictate his share of the cut; a waiter can only operate within the rules, whereas the owner makes the rules. What's the difference between someone who believes we need control and someone who believes we need service? In China, the former can get to the top of the pile, and the latter is treated like a criminal.

I'm likely to get into trouble in this altogether too free place if I take the line that Chinese people don't need to be controlled, so I can only agree with Jackie Chan's view and argue moreover that controls should be further tightened, that in the cultural sphere, for example, we should again observe taboos—not mentioning the names of our leaders, say, and replacing them with other phrases. The good news is, this advanced management system has already been implemented in many of our discussion forums. So, on this point, everyone who says Jackie Chan is talking nonsense should get arrested, on two charges: Firstly, his ideas closely correspond with those of the leaders' final speeches at the last two congresses, and secondly, they're not observing the proper taboos.

Jackie Chan said that things in Taiwan are chaotic. Now, I can't exactly contradict him, because we are supposed to figure out the majesties' intentions. *Global Times* is a paper that excels in doing just that, so when the conversation comes round to democracy in Taiwan, some of its readers will say, "Ha-ha! What kind of democracy is that? You see them cursing each other and even fighting— what a joke!"

You might think they're kidding, but they're not. Their attitude reflects the majesties' intentions, and Jackie Chan is a great reader of the majesties' intentions, too. What they say may be dumb, but it reaps dividends politically.

So on this point, too, Jackie Chan has got it right. "Things are chaotic in Taiwan" is what the people at the top have always wanted to say but felt a bit shy about saying in so many words. If Jackie Chan had been able to carry on in the direction he was moving and take things to a higher level, then he could have said, "Things in North Korea are great," or "Kim Jong-il's system of hereditary succession accords with the interests of the North Korean people," and that way he would have anticipated the leaders' thoughts to perfection. Oops, I shouldn't have said "leaders"—I'm forgetting about the taboos.

Jackie Chan also said, "Things in Hong Kong are chaotic." There seems to be a problem there—how could such an accomplished reader of minds make such a mistake? Hong Kong has already reverted to Chinese sovereignty—by now, things should be fine there. But of course the man in the street is missing the point— this is a case of profound reading of minds. It's true that Hong Kong was reclaimed in 1997, but because of Britain's brutal colonialism and cultural stranglehold, such advanced ideas as the "Two Whatevers," the "Three Represents," and the "Seven Don'ts" failed to work their magic on Hong Kong.* Because of the yawning gap between mainland and former colony, we implemented the "one country, two systems" approach, and now it's essential to establish which of the two systems is superior. What Jackie Chan is saying is, Hong Kong is not good enough, it's too free, everybody there is talking rubbish, and this is all the fault of those wicked democrats. If Hong Kong could employ the same system as the mainland, its future would be brighter. Jackie Chan is trying to strengthen our government's resolve, saying, in effect: "You should be putting Hong Kong in order, you know."

97

Jackie Chan all along has been presenting himself as a kindly big brother, and from his ideas and his participation in some activities we can see that he actually has some ambitions regarding the political arena in mainland China—greater ambitions than those in the

---

* The "Two Whatevers" policy was associated with Hua Guofeng, Mao Zedong's successor in the late 1970s, just before the reemergence of Deng Xiaoping. The "Three Represents" theory, adopted by the Chinese Communist Party in 2002, reflected the Party's effort to present itself as serving broad social interests in China. The "Seven Don'ts," first promoted in Shanghai in 1995, were injunctions against uncivilized behavior such as jaywalking and damaging public greenery.

cultural realm, and that's why, when his latest movie has just been banned in China, he still claims that Hong Kong is too free—he is really prepared to put up with a lot of aggravation if it helps him achieve his ultimate goal. Judging from his knack for anticipating his masters' wishes, I feel he has this ability, but—sad to say—I don't think he's going to end up as Minister of Propaganda or Minister of Culture, or anything like that. No matter how well he can anticipate things, the most he will ever be is a Benevolent Big Brother in the Ministry of Culture.

Why? Because his name counts against him.* It may work well for an actor, but it damages his prospects as an official. In China's feudal society it would have been thought a reactionary name, and in modern society it sounds a bit feudal. The current majesties would never allow a man with such a name to reach high office alongside them, for it sounds way too menacing. So Jackie Chan's best bet is just to continue making movies—a lot of the ones he's made I've really quite enjoyed.

As for the argument advanced by some online commentators, that Chinese people really need to be controlled, otherwise things will be in a complete mess, I think they're confusing things. Any country, any planet, needs to be managed, but what manages them shouldn't be an ideology, a system, a culture, a religion, or one's superiors, but reasonable laws and the utmost possible justice. What the people most need is to be served, not controlled, and what officials most need is to be controlled, not served, and the reason why so many places are "unharmonious" is that we have somehow got things the wrong way round. Not needing to be controlled doesn't mean giving yourself the green light to kill and loot or assault any woman you choose; what it means is that when a powerful official burns down your house, kills your children, and rapes your wife, you can make sure he gets what he deserves, rather than being

---

* Jackie Chan's Chinese name is Cheng Long, which read literally could be understood to mean, "will become a dragon."

controlled by the authorities when you appeal against the injustice, rather than having reporters muzzled and the news suppressed when you tell your story, and rather than being labeled a deranged wife-beater and falling to your death when jumping rope and ending up in the history books as a classic case of lunatic frenzy.*

---

* In February 2009, after a young man named Li Qiaoming died in police custody in Yunnan, the local authorities blamed his death on him inadvertently bumping his head against a wall when playing hide-and-seek with other prisoners. A furor erupted on the Internet, with many suspecting the death was caused by police brutality.

Further points to note about whoring

June 8, 2009

It's reported that the chief of a branch of the national tax bureau in Sichuan spent six thousand yuan to have sex with a minor. Chief Lu was held in administrative custody for fifteen days and fined five thousand yuan. The police announced, however, that his actions did not constitute a criminal offense.

On March 3 of this year, the victim, Ms. He, made a statement at Tianchi police station that on December 27, 2008, she was taken to a hotel near a hot pot restaurant in Baixi Township and there had sex with a male. Yibin Public Security investigated this as a case of suspected rape. The proprietor of the hot-pot restaurant was immediately detained, and the following day others implicated — Lu, a Mr. Xu and a Ms. Yan — were also taken into custody. That same day Lu and the restaurant proprietor were arrested, and on March 5 another suspect, surnamed Tu, was taken into custody.

Investigators established that Tu had first sought out Ms. Yan and proposed that she sell her virginity, but was turned down. Yan then relayed the same proposal to her classmate Ms. He, and introduced her to a classmate of hers named Xu. Xu put Ms. He in contact with

Tu, and on December 27, 2008, she was taken to the hot-pot restaurant by the proprietor, Tu, and others, and there introduced to Lu, for a fee of six thousand yuan; Lu then had sex with Ms. He. The restaurant proprietor pocketed two thousand yuan, while Xu, Tu, He, and others each received sums ranging from several hundred to one thousand yuan.

Yibin County Public Security Bureau met to discuss the case and concluded that the sex was a consensual act and that Lu was unaware that Ms. He was a minor under fourteen years old; Lu's actions therefore did not constitute a criminal offense. Since Lu did not know that Ms. He was or could be a minor when he paid to have sex with her, there was no case to prosecute him on those grounds.

Lessons:

1. From the case three months ago we learned that the first article of the Constitution is "If we say you're guilty, you're guilty." Now we learn the supplementary amendment to that article is "If we say you're not guilty, you're not guilty."
2. Many people get into trouble because they know too much. This bureau chief got off scot-free by pretending to know nothing.
3. From the distribution of monies to the hot-pot restaurant proprietor and the others, we see that a mere pittance is allotted to the one who takes on the most arduous duties— the lion's share goes to the middleman.
4. Relations between the various state organs in Yibin County are extremely cordial; their lines of communication are excellent.
5. Leaders in many branches of government, it is clear, have a special weakness for underage girls. As our propaganda departments would put it, this reflects their patriotism: They love our country, so they love our country's blossoms, and it's

only natural that they want to deflower them. Their actions demonstrate the utmost loyalty to the Party (and partying), so of course we're going to make sure they keep their Party affiliation.

6. Those guys who get caught with their pants down while socializing at the sauna are really unlucky. For one thing, they pay to have sex with women who are only pretending to be young, so they don't get such good value. And secondly, even though they get their kicks in spas that have paid protection money, they end up as sacrificial victims—with a six-month jail term—as a result of some dispute about profit-sharing or in response to some temporary clean-up campaign. Compared to our Mr. Lu, they really got the short end of the stick.

7. Judging from the asking price of six thousand yuan, Yibin's income levels are on the low side.

8. Men with a taste for this kind of thing will have picked up some hints on how to go about it.

The Founding of a Republic

August 8, 2009

Today I saw a list of prominent Chinese actors and performers (some of whom star in the movie *The Founding of a Republic*),* along with their current nationalities:

Chen Kaige: USA	Chen Hong: USA	Liu Yifei: USA
Joan Chen: USA	Wu Junmei: USA	Gu Changwei: USA
Jiang Wenli: USA	Hu Jing: USA	Wang Ji: USA
Lang Lang: Hong Kong	Li Yundi: France	Jiang Wen: France
Zhang Ziyi: Hong Kong	Hu Jun: Hong Kong	Tang Wei: Hong Kong
Liu Xuan: Hong Kong	Tong Ange: Canada	Xu Fan: Canada
Chen Ming: Canada	Zhang Tielin: UK	Xu Qing: Japan
Wei Wei: Germany	Shen Xiaoqin: Australia	Su Jin: New Zealand
Jet Li: Singapore	Siqin Gaowa: Switzerland	Hu Bing: Thailand.

---

* *The Founding of a Republic*, an historical drama full of cameo appearances by China's best-known actors and actresses, was released to coincide with the sixtieth anniversary of the founding of the People's Republic of China in the autumn of 2009.

That so many stars have acquired foreign passports will doubtless provoke a good deal of negative comment. "Hey, why is this?" people are bound to ask. "It was the Chinese film industry and Chinese audiences that made you famous—how can you turn out in the end to be a foreign national?"

I don't see it that way myself. Never mind the obvious benefits of having a foreign passport, like crossing borders more conveniently, enjoying greater freedom, and avoiding taxes, it seems to me that when so many artists change their nationality, their native country itself has to bear some responsibility. We hear a lot of talk about an individual's obligations, but a nation has obligations, too. It is only under exceptional circumstances that the state's legitimate interests are more important than anything else.

When so many people choose to live elsewhere, it shows that after the founding of our republic many important tasks have yet to be accomplished—otherwise, by now there would be plenty of foreigners with Chinese nationality eager to work as crew members or play the role of villainous characters in our historical dramas. For performers of Chinese origin to swap one passport for another is a choice they have made, and this choice is just like a decision to divorce—maybe it's because of irreconcilable differences or maybe because they've found a more suitable partner. Perhaps they can be reproached on moral grounds, but there is no reason to impugn their character. You can't really guarantee that you wouldn't make the same choice, can you? You there at your monitor—if offered U.S. citizenship, what would you do?

As for myself, I'm happy enough with Chinese nationality. It's true that it entails paying a great deal of tax without much to show for it and having a lot of hoops to jump through when you want to travel abroad, but that's about it.

As for the population at large, holding Chinese nationality may well mean that you can hardly afford to eat, or pay rent, or have fun, or marry, or have children, or get sick, or die, but what it means most crucially is that you can't afford to emigrate, so when people see how you lot have all flown the coop, they're bound to be pissed off.

I don't expect to change my nationality in the foreseeable future. But as you read this, don't forget that just as the nation imposes conditions on you, you can also set your own conditions on it. My condition is: It doesn't matter to me that the country I love does hardly anything at all to protect the rights of people like me in the writing profession, nor do I care that this nation turns a blind eye when the profit on the sale of any real estate property matches the income of China's biggest publishing house, but I'm very fond of children and may well not be able to restrict myself to having a single child—and certainly won't take kindly to someone from the planned-births association putting a finger on my wife—so if I'm so careless as to have one child too many, I will have to stop being a citizen of this country—or at least the mainland part of it.

"Hah, who cares what you think?" you may well say.

That's true, but I care even less what other people think. If we're so indifferent to each other's views, maybe we should just divorce. Just look at the names on the list—they all come across as decent people, no?

Report on preparations for the World Rally Championship in Australia

September 3, 2009

Several days ago I traveled from the heavenly dynasty to the island nation of Australia to monitor the preparations for the World Rally Championship. As I got off the plane, my first impression was poor: To my dismay, no reception party of primary schoolchildren pounding on waist-drums was there to greet us. And I had hardly walked a few yards before I realized that Australia is not just an island nation but a bird nation: A number of different species were roaming around as they pleased—a most unseemly spectacle.

The World Rally Championship is the world's highest-level rally competition, but in the last couple of years the Chinese Rally Championship has been advancing by leaps and bounds and promises soon to overtake it. When I arrived on the Gold Coast, the site of the rally championship, I discovered that the economy there is extremely backward. The price of a large villa with swimming pool is no more than that of a hundred-square-meter apartment in Shanghai. The local inhabitants live in wretched conditions: On the way from the airport to the hotel, I did not see a single Mercedes, BMW, or Audi, and the local government is so poor it cannot afford to erect a single toll plaza on the freeway.

When it came to tracing the rally route, there soon emerged even more compelling evidence of China's superiority. Reviewing the first stage, I found to my astonishment that members of the local animal rights association were holding up signs that read, "Go away, WRC." There are actually people there opposed to holding the rally championship! This really defies understanding. What boggles the imagination even more is that the local government can be so weak and powerless as to tolerate the conspicuous display of these placards on houses by the side of the road. I can't help but think what would happen if such unharmonious signs were to appear at our own rally championship: Not only would everyone in positions of authority down to the mayor and village head lose their jobs, but the person who dreamed up this lark could say good-bye to their monthly pension as well.

This small bunch of troublemakers, I'm told, is opposed to the rally championship on the grounds that our rally cars might hit and kill kangaroos. Little do they know that in our country hitting and killing people is not a big deal. Of course, party and government organs won't let this happen during the duration of the rally—they will give the race priority and close off the route completely. Our country's motto is: Dogs and children must be leashed; chickens and women must be penned. In our country, one hundred percent of the people support this kind of major competitive event, because those who don't support it forfeit the right to count as people—they count only as reactionaries.

After observing the low level of awareness among the local residents, I went on to inspect the other stages of the rally route, and it became apparent that the economy here is truly on its last legs. With so many farms and vacant lots sporting FOR SALE signs, people here are stone-broke. I even began to worry that a driver from China like myself might be kidnapped for ransom. All those days I was there I never saw a single policeman, which goes to show how weak the forces of law and order are. The only way to protect myself was to announce at every opportunity that back in China I am neither a member of the Communist Party nor a real estate developer.

Speaking of police, when the Chinese Rally Championship is held, the government gives it enormous attention, assigning up to a thousand policemen to manage traffic in the vicinity and maybe sending in military police and infantry for good measure; even a hen that strays onto the race route will be summarily shot. But the Australian government has clearly failed to allocate adequate management resources. I didn't see a single policeman along the whole three-hundred-kilometer route, but I did spot a snake as thick as a man's thigh wriggling across the road, which gave the driver a great fright. Competitors with a fear of reptiles will be unable to perform at their top level or exhibit their best style.

The World Rally Championship referees are a shabby lot. On a route inspection in China, there's no need to consult the map—just look out for the police sentry stations and you'll be on the right road, and you'll find the referee station where there's a big clump of people. It's all very imposing. But at the WRC I couldn't see any referees at the spot marked on the map—I had to get out of the car and ask an elderly couple who were having a picnic where I could find them. It turned out *they* were the referees! Can't they do better than that?

On the second leg, it was a similar situation—a pair of lovers under an umbrella. I thought at first they were fishing! They offered me a piece of candy, but I remembered the education I received as a youngster—this had to be a capitalist sugar-coated bullet, so I refused it.

Preparations for the special stages were a complete bomb. The competitive stage that I visited was due to take place on a city thruway. I got there at 6:30, but even by 7:30 the road had not been closed off. How can they be so sloppy in their urban management work? Don't they know that without some brisk beatings of drivers who dare to encroach on the rally route (state-owned property, after all!), one will never be able to seal off a roadway promptly? If this kind of competition were held in our country, three days before the race the road would have been closed, and both sides of the road would be given a new coat of paint—and the grass would be given a new coat of paint, too. That'd be sure to give the drivers an excellent impression, and demonstrate our government's consistently strong posture—toward its own people, that is.

Although the competition has yet to begin, I can tell you right now that the international car league and the Chinese car league are not at all on the same level. Competitions abroad only make a fuss about inspections—because my driving shoes had a hole in them, for example, I almost failed the inspection. In China, on the other hand, you're completely free to compete in a race wearing dress shoes. Our car inspections just involve checking the manufacturer—if you apply to drive a Subaru, say, and turn up in a Subaru and not on a kangaroo, then you will pass the inspection just fine. There's plenty of wiggle room on stuff like engine displacement, upgrade, and model. The international standard of inspection is simply too rigid, too lacking in flexibility: It doesn't allow enough room for individual preferences and wreaks havoc with one's profits. Also, every time I go somewhere in China, the local leadership warmly greets me and expresses the hope that I'll help promote the development of the local economy. "Sure," I tell them, "I'll be happy to take a picture of the city government offices and post it online to show how well you're doing." I don't know why, but they always modestly decline this offer. But I spent a full three days in Australia, and never had the chance to meet the local leadership. I feel this is a shocking breach of etiquette. Most discourteous of all—I was never able to locate their local government offices, for I often mistook them for portable toilets. A country like this, so indifferent to the image of its government—how could it ever run a proper competition?

Australia's World Rally Championship is staring failure in the face. On China's behalf, I invite the Australian rally stages to shift their location to China. I can guarantee you will find absolutely no "unharmonious" phenomena here. Instead, there will be cars to drive, meals to savor, cash to spend, and whores to bed. Of course, if you take a fancy to our country and get the idea of living there permanently, better forget that—there's no way you can afford to buy one of our homes.

November 21, 2009

The day before yesterday I gave a little speech at the Jiading Expo Forum. Normally I never attend any forums whatsoever, but the organizers made a very earnest appeal and on September 30 even came in person to deliver the invitation—and gave me a little present to boot. For me to receive a gift from the Party and the state on the eve of National Day came as such a surprise that I decided to set aside my principles and accept the invitation. I made a point of preparing my remarks in advance, fearing I might say something out of turn if I ad-libbed. "This is the first time I ever heard of you ever giving a formal lecture," a friend said to me. "I don't want to miss it." He sat down in front of his computer to watch the live video feed.

So there, thirty miles away, I introduced my theme—"The city makes life more miserable" * and expressed the view that for most people the pressure of life in Shanghai is becoming unbearable. After the talk I asked my friend what he thought. "Hell," he said, "the broadcast went dead as soon as you announced your topic."

---

* The official theme of the 2010 Shanghai Expo was "Better City, Better Life"—or, more literally in Chinese, "The city makes life more beautiful."

Those of you who want to read the full text are just going to have to wait.

This reminds me that a few days ago the U.S. Embassy called me up. When President Obama visits Shanghai there will be a chance for him to interact with young Chinese, and they asked if I'd like to take part in the dialogue. I declined, saying I had a race that day. Actually, whether it is the American president or the Chinese one, there's nothing I particularly need to ask or say. But the main thing is, I have absolutely no interest in sharing a room with a bunch of actors, that's all.

Try the pickles

December 14, 2009

One thing I have learned from our nation's news coverage is that we have a the great variety of government departments, and the one I've been informed about now is the National Standards Commission. After long focusing only on internal matters and determining that the cost of an official's meal must not exceed one hundred thousand yuan, that an official cannot keep more than five mistresses or engage more than two prostitutes at a time, and that an official cannot pocket a single bribe larger than one hundred million yuan, the National Standards Commission has now set its sights and its antennae on the common people, and has stipulated that a battery-powered bicycle cannot exceed a speed of fifteen to twenty kilometers an hour or a weight of forty kilos, otherwise it will be treated as a motor vehicle.

How did this standard come into being? It's simple. Businessmen make money from new products, and the government makes money from new policies. With the implementation of this standard, most battery-powered bicycles will be designated light motorcycles or electric motorcycles (a novel expression, that!), and their license fees and sales tax will see an enormous increase. I don't quite get it: If the relevant departments are introducing this change in the name of protecting lives, then how is it that those heavier or faster bicycles suddenly become safer just because they command more exorbitant fees?

In this reform we can see the authorities' determination to get their pound of flesh. They know that those cunning people whose bicycles can speed along at forty kilometers an hour are quite capable of making technical adjustments so that they will go only twenty or even fifteen kilometers an hour during the inspection, and then the authorities won't be able to get their hands on that extra cash. So what do they do? They come out with the forty-kilo weight limit, because heavy bikes are bound to be able to go faster, and now there's no escaping the extra expense. My suggestion to working people is that if their bike really does exceed the limits, then when the inspection is scheduled you simply detach the heavy electric battery and the tires and whatnot, and tell the inspectors that because you trust the government and trust the state, then not only will you not die riding the bike, but you can even ride it without power and without wheels.

A price has to be paid for any kind of transport, and for a long time, in the name of safety, the government has restricted the use of motorcycles. In other countries, lots of young guys just out of high school depend on a motorbike as they start a career, and for many less well-off families a motorbike is an indispensable accessory when going out—you can't insist that everyone always take public transport, after all. Later, of those who used to buy motorbikes, some chose to take the bus or the subway, some bought small cars, some bought e-bikes. Now ticket prices and gasoline prices have gone up, and in some places license and road-use fees are levied for cars, but the authorities have had a hard time making money out of those low-income e-bike users—even if electricity rates rise, the money goes into other people's pockets. So now the principles of fairness and justice come into effect, and now it's the e-bike riders turn to pay up.

Well, are e-bikes safe? No, they're not. That's because they run silently and brake poorly, even though they can reach or exceed speeds of fifty kilometers an hour. But it's rare for an e-bike to knock someone down and kill them—it's much more common for an e-bike rider to get killed in a collision, and the new standards are going to do nothing to reduce the casualties from that kind of accident. The norm for e-bikes is actually very simple: there should be no charge for their registration and license, their speed should be limited to thirty-five to forty kilometers per hour, they must have disc brakes, and their riders must wear a helmet. The disc brakes are especially vital. A lot of e-bikes, including many of those that can go over fifty kilometers an hour, have much the same brake system as a comparable light motorcycle: They are all fitted with disc brakes, and I find that reassuring. It shows that though these manufacturers may not excel in basic technology, their basic sense of decency compares well with that of some official departments—that's to say, if you spend more, you will get a higher level of service and accessories. This is not to deny that it's still a bit dangerous for an e-bike to exceed fifty kilometers an hour: It's not equipped with great tires, and it makes so little noise that it can do considerable damage to a pedestrian if it hits one at that kind of speed.

A neighbor of mine works in a plant at the Jinshan Petroleum works near Shanghai, and his commute involves a twenty-five-kilometer bus ride. But often he's asked to work overtime, and the bus is no longer running when he gets off work. His monthly salary is 1,650 yuan—pretty good pay, by local standards. He wanted to buy a motorbike and liked the look of one that cost over four thousand yuan. "I have one just like that," I said to him, "that I've only ridden a hundred kilometers. I'll sell it to you for one thousand yuan." (If you're wondering why I didn't just give it to him for free, use your brain.) A month later he said, "I don't want your bike anymore. I have to pay for a license, and what's worse, the fuel costs are too much—four or five hundred yuan a month, I just can't afford it. See this e-bike I've got—it can go fifty kilometers an hour, too."

Once the new standard comes into effect, it's hard to know how my friend will manage. He's got two choices. One, he spends a little money, rides his "electric motorcycle" for half an hour to get home, and if his luck holds out, lives to a ripe old age. Two, he trades in his bike for one that meets the national standard and takes two hours to get home each day, rain or shine, with the risk that he won't have enough power to get himself home.

E-bikes are the mode of transport for the second-poorest members of the community. These people are always running around to make ends meet, and while you don't want them to risk their lives by riding at breakneck speed, you can't expect them to get things done at a snail's pace. In any case, I think it's unreasonable for the authorities to try to squeeze more money out of them. Some people eat abalone, but just because they see others eat too many pickles they can't set a standard and say, you've got to eat this set amount of pickles each day and no more, otherwise you'll damage your health. Their solution to the problem is not to replace the pickles with meat, but rather charge the poor pickle-eaters for the pickles that they have overeaten or are about to overeat, at the market rate for meat. But, if you think people are so happy to eat pickles, you should eat one yourself and see. Of course, if you eat pickles once in a blue moon you might think they're delicious, just like that provincial administrator who rode a bike to work in the car lane once and thought it was great. If you're really such hot stuff, how about you eat pickles every day?

Just testing

January 15, 2010

Recently I read several reports about Shanghai; I think it's worth reviewing them here. First of all, Shanghai's bulldozers are pressing forward with urban construction at a rate of practically one crushed person a day. If they carry on at this rate, the China Pavilion at the Shanghai Expo will be stained red with more than just paint.

Secondly, the director of the Shanghai politics and law commission has declared that criminal syndicates will never be allowed to establish themselves in Shanghai. That's an issue that has never caused me anxiety, because the cost of living in Shanghai is so high that no kingpin can afford to support a gang. Shanghai has found a supremely effective means to deny gangs a foothold here.

Thirdly, the Shanghai government has announced that when necessary it will implement measures to restrict car usage, such as stipulating that only vehicles whose license plates end with odd or even numbers can enter the city on a particular day. They got the idea from Beijing, which introduced this system during the 2008 Olympics. But in Beijing a license only costs two hundred yuan, and there's no congestion fee. Cars licensed in Shanghai have license fees of anything from thirty thousand to forty thousand yuan, and gas prices here are significantly higher than in other cities, as well. You take people's money, but then not only do you not get things done, you make life difficult for the people whose money you pocket. Oh, and I almost forgot—we need to fork out another eighteen hundred yuan to cover that highway-loan surcharge. It sure seems odd to me that when we're the ones who make the down payment and we're the ones who pay off the loan—with all the interest going to you—we get to use the road only at fixed times.

This new rule won't have any impact on me, since I spend most of my time out in the countryside and rarely venture into the city. But if in the future they really go ahead and limit car use, I think people won't have much alternative but to just leave their cars in the road and go back home. The government can restrict access because the roads are too congested, but we can't restrict our leaders from going to work just because they are so stupid.

122 Also, many people have asked me what I think about Google closing its operations in China. When Google Library was scanning the works of Chinese authors, a reporter asked me my reaction to Google's scanning my books without permission and putting them online for people to read for free, giving me sixty dollars at most in compensation. What I told him was, if this is what Google is really doing, that explains why it hasn't managed to gain the biggest share of the Chinese market. Only when I got home and went online did I find out that Google had been scanning only the table of contents. Then I realized why Google hadn't captured a larger market share—too many people have been demonizing it. Actually, whether or not it's true that Google is pulling out of China, I understand its position. The thing I don't understand is the online survey that claims seventy percent of those polled do not support Google's demand that the Chinese government remove its filters from online search results. When you look at the poll results on government websites, you have to wonder why you so often find yourself at odds with public opinion, and after many such experiences you must

begin to suspect that you're a member of the 1990s generation, to always be so out of the mainstream. Actually, it's the government websites that should be blocked. I can live with black being called gray and white being called cream, but I can't tolerate a complete reversal of black and white.

If Google leaves China, the people who should most be wringing their hands are writers. This is not because Chinese writers represent society's conscience and progressive tendencies, for many of them do not care about the limits on expression, and even if the government departments overseeing culture were to block a full half of the Chinese characters in circulation, writers would still find a way of using the remaining vocabulary to sing the authorities' praises. What *will* upset them is that if they had known Google was going to run out on them, they would have definitely accepted those sixty dollars, for this would surely be the first income most Chinese authors have gained in terms of electronic publishing rights. All they wanted, really, was another forty dollars, to make a nice round one hundred.

Finally, I read a report that in the future if a cell phone forwards a dirty joke or some indecent content, the messaging function on that phone will be disabled and you'll have to go to Public Security and sign a promise of good behavior before you can regain messaging capability. That's the government for you: It is always coming out with some verb or noun but never explains what that word means. You're not to be counterrevolutionary, it says, for instance, without defining *counterrevolutionary*. You can't be a hooligan, it says, but it won't tell you what a *hooligan* is. Now, you can't send an indecent message but it won't say what it means by *indecent*. I'd like to follow the government's lead but am stymied when it gives me no clear standard to follow. The result is that some of us step into a minefield without realizing it, and even those Fifty-centers suffer embarrassment when they try their best to suck up to the powers that be only to have their messages rejected as problematic. My suggestion is: with these minefields, You should tell us clearly—this is a minefield here, and if you enter you'll be responsible for the consequences. But not only do you not put up a sign to warn us away from the minefield, you lay mines under the pedestrian crossing. Whose fault is it if one of those mines goes off?

Given that we're coming up to the Chinese New Year, so as to avoid phone users losing access to their phones just when they're so busy and having to go to the police station on the first day of the New Year, I have decided to sacrifice myself: In the days to come I plan to constantly forward indecent messages of various kinds, until my cell phone has been disabled. After that happens, I will finally be able to tell you what constitutes an indecent message. So, if any of you receive dirty messages from me in the next few days, don't get the wrong idea. It's not that I'm getting horny or trying to make a move on you—I'm just testing.

Required course for
Chinese officials: Lesson One

January 20, 2010

As someone has remarked, the main contradiction in China today is that between the growing intelligence of the population at large and the rapidly waning morality of our officials. But as our officials' moral sense crumbles, their judgment, managerial ability, command of Chinese, personal appeal, and competence in a crisis are in constant decline as well. After many years of observation I realize that many things are actually not a problem to begin with, but once officials start to intervene, a small thing becomes big, and the big thing blows up in their faces and ends up a major talking point. Here I propose to outline some common-sense approaches that will help leaders at all levels handle issues correctly, so that they can get promoted and make more money more quickly. Here begins Lesson One.

According to a report by Gansu Province's news website, Gansu is about to establish a team of six hundred and fifty Internet commenters to lead public opinion in the right direction. The Gansu authorities originally planned to promote this as a major political achievement, hoping for some reward from their superiors. Various branches of the provincial government held a meeting in Lanzhou specifically to discuss this issue, and thus a press release was circulated to the outside world.

On the Internet we often see people talking about "the tragedy of Lanzhou"—although the Gansu provincial leadership probably has no clue what they're talking about. Now we see a Lanzhou tragedy unroll before our eyes. The Gansu report was initially posted on major news websites, but when opening these web pages today I found that all the links to this item have been frozen—not one of them can be opened. Who has been "harmonizing" the Propaganda Department, one wonders? The Propaganda Department Central Office, of course. The leaders of Gansu Province, alas, have done a lousy job of interpreting the imperial will. This time they've really put their foot in it with their misguided effort to curry favor.

126

The other name for Internet commenters is "the fifty-cent party"—hired hands who masquerade as ordinary Internet users— really a variety of mole. It's a colossal mistake to make public the placement and identity of moles. This information should have been passed on to the higher authorities in the form of a secret document delivered by a special agent. Doing that would certainly have elicited a handsome reward. But by publicizing this story, Gansu has laid bare a fact that the government has always been unwilling to admit—the existence of the "fifty-cent party." If someone has to spend money to buy praise and support, that's a sure sign that he's got a lousy record. This news has directly shattered the false image that the higher authorities have worked so hard to create. I think we can be sure that the leaders of the Gansu propaganda department have not a hope in hell of ever getting promoted now.

According to the report, Gansu Province must speed up its surveillance of the Internet this year and establish an Internet commenter team, a system in which fifty commentary experts form the core, augmented by one hundred commentary talents, with five hundred commentary writers constituting the outer circle.

If a small province like Gansu needs to hire another six hundred and fifty Internet commenters, it's not hard for those with curious minds to work out that in the nation as a whole there must be at least one hundred thousand people whose full-time job it is to post comments on the Internet. If we assume that each commenter's annual salary is fifty thousand yuan, then the government's annual expenditure on complimenting itself must come to five billion yuan, which is equivalent to twenty-five thousand Hope Primary Schools, or one-tenth of the cost of the Three Gorges Dam, or more or less the cost of the two new Shanghai bridges across the Huangpu River plus the bill for constructing the Oriental Pearl, or thirty Boeing 737s, or a medium-sized aircraft carrier, or ninety of those Mil Mi-26 helicopters that we were in desperate need of after the Wenchuan earthquake and had to resort to borrowing from Russia. If these figures were by any chance to be leaked, this could easily create friction between the people and the government!

It's human nature to make oneself look good by sticking gold leaf on one's face, and it's obviously going to cost money to do that, but if you're trying to stick an aircraft carrier on your face, this shows the face you have is really getting way too big. The good thing is that none of those busybodies has yet got round to adding up all these figures and nobody has yet sounded the alarm, so we can all rest easy.

From this Lanzhou tragedy, you officials will see there's a very thin line between understanding and misunderstanding your superiors' wishes. Propaganda departments far and near, take heed.

Are you Xiaoming?

February 6, 2010

I wonder if you've noticed that there's been an increase recently in the number of Fifty-centers appearing in the main online forums and news discussions. Of course, I'm not in favor of labeling as Fifty-centers everyone who disagrees with you, but Fifty-centers are easy to spot, because people who sell their souls—particularly people who sell their souls at such a low price—will say things that have no basis and will climax without any foreplay. When I first noticed the proliferation of Fifty-centers, I was quite perplexed and thought it must be because the authorities had increased their budget, but later I read a report that attributed it to the economic crisis. Recently Section 5, Clause 17 of a document entitled "Internet Commenters' Management Methods," issued by the Communist Party network in the city of Hengyang, stipulates that the standard remuneration for Internet commenters is ten cents per post. It's pretty obvious that, nationwide, the Fifty-centers have seen a reduction in their pay, and that helps to explain why we have the sensation that all of a sudden there are five times as many of them as there used to be. Actually, it's just the same number of people, but they're all working overtime. In the past, when we spotted a Fifty-center, we could all gather round and peer at him, but now, with forum administrators deleting our posts and other Internet users chiming in with their own comments, we sometimes find ourselves totally outnumbered by Fifty-centers.

According to that top-secret Gansu document on "The Composition of Fifty-centers," their ranks are staffed by fifty skilled writers, one hundred competent writers, and five hundred outer-circle writers. The Fifty-centers whose comments we see everywhere are, so far as I can tell, made up largely of the outer-circle writers, but from time to time a few "competent writers" emerge to test the waters. As for the "skilled writers," I suspect they must have other administrative responsibilities, for we haven't seen much sign of them. Of course, the main reason for their absence is that they're busy attending banquets and raking in gifts during the Chinese New Year.

The recent proliferation of Fifty-centers is one of the reasons I started my microblog. For one thing, the Fifty-centers react rather slowly to new things, and I'm sure that for many "competent writers," just registering and signing in to the Tencent web browser is already as much as they can manage. At the same time, one can't express views anonymously on a microblog, and that makes them scared to register. And most importantly, if by any chance they perform conspicuously well on the microblog front and their superiors direct them to consolidate their position, they'd have to tie themselves to their cell phone in order to constantly manipulate public opinion, and that would be their ruin. They're only getting paid ten cents per post, after all, and it costs the same amount to send out a text message; if you factor in the cost of recharging their phone battery, then just for them to break even would be a sheer impossibility. You shouldn't make fun of them—they sell their souls for ten cents and would sell a kidney for a thousand yuan, so for them even the tiniest fraction of a yuan is a significant gain or loss. Although ideologically they align themselves most impeccably with the ruling class, their actual livelihood places them at the bottom of the social pyramid.

I think we should permit the Fifty-centers to exist, for everyone has the right to hire others to speak on their behalf, and every hired worker has the right to speak wherever they please. If you can give Xiaoming a beating and then hire someone else with the money you've pilfered from Xiaoming's pocket to give Xiaoming a scolding, that just shows you've got a good deal of gumption. Every government has an agency that helps to promote it, and that's perfectly understandable. But the Fifty-centers are a fiasco. I used to think that they served to shape public opinion but now I realize that's not so, because nobody who sees a crowd of people standing around eating shit is going to try to squeeze their way in and eat it, too. The Fifty-centers originally were a product of provincial governments trying to curry favor with the top leadership. But now, with so many Fifty-centers on the loose, lots of "upstanding" and "correct" people may simply open their mouths—clearly without getting paid a cent—and they immediately are written off as Fifty-centers, so this has gravely damaged their enthusiasm. You check into a hotel for a one-night stand and when you come out everyone thinks you're a prostitute—this has to be a bit demoralizing. Once you institute this Fifty-center structure, apart from the damage done to your image both domestically and overseas, all of your original supporters end up suspected of being Fifty-centers.

Why do I seldom have good words for our government? One reason is that I don't want other people saying I'm a Fifty-center; a second is that when one has no freedom to criticize, then praise is meaningless; and the third is that I've already paid my taxes, and our taxes are used to foot the bill for the Fifty-centers' expenses, so that is equivalent to me indirectly praising the government.

Finally, I plan to sift through a batch of posts and differentiate which ones were written by the outer circle, which by the competent writers, which by patriotic youth, which by ignorant young girls, which by unhappy people, and which by idiots. If I put you in the wrong category, and your comment was purely voluntary and not for profit, there's really nothing I can do about that. You should ask your masters why a view like yours could be worth a full ten cents.

Han Feng is a fine cadre

March 4, 2010

In recent days the diary kept by Han Feng, a director in the Laibin Tobacco Bureau, has become a big sensation.* In an era where the Internet is flooded with pinups and videos, I find it refreshing to suddenly encounter such an authentic piece of writing—surely it will go down in history as the work with the greatest literary and social value to be released in China in 2010. Assuming that the diary is genuine, I'm confident that it establishes its author as a fine cadre, for the following reasons:

1. This cadre accepted only sixty thousand yuan in bribes during a six-month period—the first time in several years that I've seen only five figures associated with the word *bribes*. Where else could one find such an honest bureau chief?

---

* Between November 2009 and February 2010 there appeared online extracts from the diary of Han Feng, director of the Laibin Tobacco Bureau in Guangxi. In them, Han Feng candidly recorded his daily activities, including sex bouts with his mistresses. On March 13, 2010, he was arrested on charges of corruption and subsequently expelled from the Communist Party.

2. Of the women he has had affairs with or is currently conducting affairs with, not one has been elevated to full-blown second-wife status.

3. This bureau chief does not gamble or go whoring or bribe his superiors. When purchasing a cell phone, he waited in line like everyone else and it took him two hours to complete his purchase.

4. In the pages of the diary, we find a state official who chases skirt with the least possible financial outlay. At a time when other officials regularly buy their mistresses an automobile or an apartment, the most expensive present he ever gives one of his women is a cell phone or an MP4 player. This shows not only that Han Feng is a decent fellow but that his partners are decent women, too. If there were more couples like this in our country, we could easily afford to build several more aircraft carriers.

5. He attended banquets on only eighty-nine occasions, when I know of many village officials whose banquets over the course of a year number well over three hundred and sixty-five. But he often got drunk, which reflects a poor capacity for alcohol, so in this area he has fallen well short of the standards expected of an official. This has to constitute his gravest offense, for here he has seriously sullied the reputation of our civil servants.

6. Although he sported with women on multiple occasions, he also accompanied his wife on shopping or other excursions on twenty-five days and bought his father a cell phone. There is no evidence that he used his authority to advance the interests of family members.

7. He knows how to install computer software, loves digital technology, photography, and sports, and is capable of using microblog services to maintain his diary; this all shows that he is an official capable of keeping abreast of the latest developments.

8. In his diary we see not the slightest sign of a desire to own luxury cars or expensive property or paintings, calligraphy, and antiques; all he does is quietly do stuff on his cell phone and computer. In his diary he even writes, "Today I spent one hundred sixty yuan on a pair of headphones—they're terrific." What a modest, easy-to-please official!
9. As for his job performance—although we have yet to uncover evidence of him doing any work, given that he is a bureau chief who has burrowed his way inside a number of female subordinates, his title and his performance more or less match.

To sum up, in the current scheme of things Han Feng is undoubtedly a more than satisfactory official, one who amuses himself with harmless pursuits, one who refrains from excess, one who inflicts no suffering on the people and little damage on the state. In this diary we find an official who is over the moon with a purchase of just a few thousand yuan, who, after buying a new cell phone, for three days straight makes one and the same diary entry: "Fooled around at home with my new phone." He was so happy he even gave up on fooling around with women! I strongly suggest that we let him off and give his lady friends a break as well, for they are but the tiniest of little shrimp and their biggest sin has been simply to have nibbled on some floating organic matter as they paddle about in the water. We can hope that functionaries like Han Feng will be punished for their offenses, but we certainly should not regard them as the incarnations of official malfeasance. In an official culture where decadence is the norm, they have to count as the most innocuous, environmentally friendly elements. We should let this bureau chief remain in his position and allow him to continue researching his digital products. If he is dismissed from office, his successor is likely to be a bigger threat to society, for the simple reason that he will know not to keep a diary.

135

Where else could I find
someone like you?

March 14, 2010

Since I set up my public opinion poll, some 210,000 Internet users have registered their votes, and of these, ninety-six percent think Han Feng is a fine civil servant and should retain his position, and only four percent think he is a bad one and should be punished. In the future I plan to conduct other such polls, as a way of compensating for no one ever having seen an electoral ballot, despite all those elections of representatives to the National People's Congress. Starting today, I am unilaterally setting myself up as a strategic collaboration partner to the major governmental websites, so that when they invite participation in some poll or other, I will do the same (but refraining from writing anything that might shape voters' views on the subject), and then see how my poll results compare with theirs.

Among the voters, some feel strongly that Han Feng is really not bad at all, given that his appetite is so limited, and some profess a genuine respect for his decency as an official, while others are mocking or ironic in their comments, but all are conscious that this is a matter completely out of their hands. In my grandfather's younger days, when everyone was in economic difficulties, local officials were not necessarily any better off, and only later did it become clear that in our country there was a stark distinction between good officials and bad officials. The result of the Han Feng poll shows that we have entered a new era, one in which there is hardly a single official with clean hands, in which it's only a matter of good corrupt officials and bad corrupt officials. People believe overwhelmingly that Han Feng belongs to the first category.

Although Han Feng was recently arrested on a charge of accepting bribes during real estate transactions, when reading reports about him we shouldn't just focus on his fondness for tinkering with technology, abusing his office, and taking liberties with women. In an interview with *New Century Weekly*, one of Han Feng's superiors said, "Tobacco consumption in Guangxi seriously lags behind other provinces. One of Han Feng's achievements was to raise consumption in his area of jurisdiction to over six cartons per capita, exceeding the nationwide average."

138

In this admirable part of the country, then, people originally did not smoke very much. So the government set up an agency which had the mission of raising tobacco consumption; success in pulling off this assignment is one of the criteria for identifying an effective leader, and inducing ordinary people to smoke more has become a feat about which a government agency feels proud. It's bad enough for a respectable country to not prohibit smoking—how can you sacrifice public health just for a tiny boost in GDP? But then, when I think about it, there's nothing strange about that—it's been the pattern all along.

When the National People's Congress and the National Political Consultative Conference were in session, reporters were always asking if I had any legislation I'd like to propose, or suggested I record some interviews about people's lives today, or even go to Beijing and mingle with some of the delegates, but I turned all these invitations down. As someone in absolutely no position of authority, what could

I hope to achieve? And besides, for one thing, I can communicate my ideas well enough, just using my laptop; and, for another, I've made it clear already that I'm not into putting on a show.

But now, as those two meetings come to an end, the point I want to make is that our government is really very fortunate. A majority of people always take the view that the top leadership's policies are correct, but are simply mishandled by administrators lower down — never do they question the first part of that proposition. They continue to cling to the most primitive trust in our top leaders. When ordinary citizens encounter mistreatment, their final resort is to go to the capital to denounce their persecutors, although the Letters and Visits Office's main order of business is simply to add their names to the list of targets of security monitoring and send them back where they came from. When they're abused by the village chief they appeal to the township chief, and when the township chief pays them no attention they appeal to the district chief, and when the district chief will have nothing to do with them they appeal to the city mayor, but they have no hope of ever securing an audience with him, and so they fantasize about finding the sympathetic ear of a minister in the central government (or someone even higher up), convinced that these lower-level leaders have blocked the transmission of their complaint. The possibility seems to have never occurred to them that the person they most want to see decided long ago that they were an infernal nuisance, rejecting their petition with an offhand "He's failing to see the full picture." All they ever seek is a little benefit, never insisting that they have a certain right; they always feel the problem lies with the local officials and nowhere else. Just as long as some big-shot in an Audi extends a greeting at the Chinese New Year, they get a warm sensation inside. They feel an official like Han Feng is really doing a pretty good job, for their hope is not that a functionary will serve the common people, but simply that he won't cause trouble for them. You can live in your fine apartment, drive your nice car, screw your little secretary, and we won't object to any of that. So long as you don't beat up my son, demolish my little home, or molest my daughter, you count as a good official in the eyes of the people. If bloggers annoy you, you can delete their posts; if writers antagonize you, you can harmonize them; if journalists displease you, you can deal with them in just one short line: "No negative reporting allowed."

So, as I say, our government is fortunate to have a population that is so simple and kind-hearted and so easy to satisfy. Although they have many gripes, they also have a basic level of trust. Occasionally they may stir up a fuss, but at the most that's because you originally promised to let them have a meat bun if they gave you all their cake, and then you only actually give them a plain bun. All you need to do is pick up a toothpick and dislodge a shred of meat from between your molars to give them as filling for their bun, and they will go home quite contentedly. When dealing with the populace, I really wish the government could forget all the hoopla surrounding GDP and be a bit more accommodating. At your meetings, please recite fewer of those elegantly phrased epigrams and allocate everyone a bigger bowl of soup, subject people to less pressure in their lives, protect them, look out for them, and let them have a little dignity of their own, rather than letting dignity reside only with a notice from the New China News Agency. If you let such a wonderful people die of starvation or illness or poverty or despair or air pollution or toxic food products or rage or mistreatment or contaminated water, or "sleep," wherever are you are going to find another population?

Letters from strangers

———————————

April 4, 2010

Ever since a newspaper article provided independent travelers with directions to my hometown, a number of visitors have managed to find their way there, and sometimes they bring little gifts or drop off a few pictures. But recently people have been delivering letters—with messages that leave me feeling helpless and distressed.

In Imperial China, when ordinary people suffered injustice at the hands of local officials, they would go to the capital to complain directly to the pinnacle of power. The lucky ones might be able to intercept the sedan chair of an official; the most fortunate of all might manage to run into the emperor himself as he traveled about in disguise. These outcomes, however improbable, served psychologically to support society's yearning for equity and justice. In modern times, leaders have exchanged sedan chairs for luxury automobiles, and trying to stop one of their vehicles would be completely suicidal, and top leaders have so much exposure on television that they can't possibly go out incognito on inspection tours. Even when they visit the countryside, all that happens is that they go on a photo shoot arranged by the local officials where they conduct a performance in conjunction with some peasant showmen, but that's all just make-believe—it has next to nothing to do with ordinary folk. These days, the Letters and Visits Office is the only recourse for most people who have been treated unjustly.

Clearly, the people are way too naïve: In a country where the judiciary has no independence, how can you expect that a branch of government will suddenly come to your defense? If another kid slaps you and his mom scolds you and his dad punches you in the face, when you go running to the granddad to complain about his terrible offspring, you should know perfectly well that the best you can hope for is a kick in the shin. Even if that sign in the cavernous lobby of their office building says something to the effect that they're "here to serve you," they just put that up there because they think the calligraphy makes a nice fashion statement, and you should never mistake that old saw for their guiding philosophy.

So, once people realize that petitioning for redress not only gets them nowhere but actually amounts to putting their own names on the blacklist and subjecting themselves to more abuse, more and more they begin to turn to the media. Journalists, after all, although hamstrung by all kinds of bans and prohibitions, do have professional ideals and will battle against injustice to the extent that's possible. In the same way, race car drivers have the goal of driving fast, and actors try to play their parts convincingly, but I'm really unclear what government functionaries see as their professional ideal. Maybe it's simply to eat and drink to their hearts' content, to loaf about, to look out for their big break, to trim their sails to the wind, so that in the end they enjoy a smooth ride through officialdom, with the power and position and gray income* accruing thereto. Precisely because they have no proper professional ideals, they have no professional accomplishments. Basically, in their eyes, petitioners are just troublemakers who fail to show due deference to the big picture.

---

* Income from bribes, embezzlement, and corruption.

Many people who have suffered unfair treatment associate me with the media and hope I will take up their cause and write something on their behalf so that their predicament attracts attention. I can do nothing for them, however. Their misfortunes are a heavy burden to them, but possess little news value to the media, and I'm sure that even if I were to write something about it the traditional media wouldn't pay any attention. But the resolution of an issue very often requires their help; only then will leaders come forth in a big song-and-dance to respond to the people's needs and identify with their grievances. A common complaint I hear is about the poor quality of housing provided to displaced city residents, with a landfill or a transformer substation just around the corner; another is that people's houses have been forcibly demolished. But for your home to be demolished without your consent doesn't count as news—in China, that is life. If you managed to avoid getting burned to a cinder and are still able to send and receive e-mail and all your family members are still alive, that counts as a happy life and you should thank the state for allowing you such a favorable outcome.

143

The most tragic letter I received was sent from the provinces, with loads of supporting documentation. A family had been forcibly evicted, and some of its members had been injured. Most of their house had been categorized as an illegal building. They went to Beijing to submit an appeal, and the result was that their supporting materials were sent back to the province, and from there to the municipality, and from there to the county, and from there to the village, and thereafter, whenever a national holiday came round, the whole family would be placed under watch by a community policing team, to prevent them from damaging the harmonious atmosphere. In the end they took the case to court and, much to their surprise, the judges agreed to hear it.

When I read that, I was astonished, too. Aren't the courts simply service organizations for the government? How could they handle this case? I couldn't wait to turn over the page.

What the next page told me is that the court reached a verdict very quickly: Originally it had been agreed that the government would compensate the victims to the tune of two hundred thousand yuan, but the verdict now was that the government need only pay out one hundred thousand yuan.

The main reason why I can't give the full details of these cases is that I have not verified all the facts, and that is something beyond my power to do. But I'm confident that the letters are largely, or even entirely, truthful—for, at most, their authors have added a few details to give more weight to their case, without affecting the main facts of the matter—and there's no question that their adversaries are screwing them over. In the face of these begging letters, I feel entirely powerless. Of course, they are not expecting that I will right all their wrongs—they simply want to explore every possible avenue of redress.

The people who are in the direst need of all most likely are quite unable to appeal. They have appealed to government functionaries, only to find that apart from functionaries there is nobody else who is abusing them. So they appeal to the Communist Party organization, only to find that the organization is made up of functionaries big and small, so then they go looking for the Letters and Visits Office, only to find that this simply facilitates their monitoring by the public security organs, and finally they go to court and pay the fee for filing an appeal, and all along this road they are confronted by hostile forces, so then they try something different: the media, only to discover that there are too many people in equally bad shape and that their own suffering is not sufficiently grave to make news, so then they try the Internet, where they discover that unlucky devils are a dime a dozen and that their own bad luck is not so very unique and has failed to plumb the very lowest depths of human misery. What, then, can they do?

What is it you're so afraid of?

April 17, 2010

Today, through some chat rooms, I heard about the three people who have been sentenced to jail terms in Mawei, Fujian. To be honest, this was complete news to me, so I began a search. First of all I tried Google's Hong Kong site, only to find that it was just like if you try to search for "carrot" or "plum"—the page simply refused to open.* So then I tried the Baidu search engine, and all I learned is that these three netizens had been arrested on suspicion of slander. *Who was it they slandered?* I wondered. *If they slandered the local public security agency,* I thought, *then it's all over for them.* For when they slander the local public security, and their case is then handled by the local courts—well, won't they have already agreed on the sentence when they all have dinner together in a local restaurant?

In the interests of being fair to all parties, I continued my search for a report on how these three netizens had slandered the govern-

---

* At various times, Chinese users of Google have found that searches for "carrot" and other seemingly innocuous words trigger error messages, since these terms may share characters with names of China's top leaders. The character *hu* in Hu Jintao, for example, also appears in the word for "carrot."

ment, but the trail soon went cold. First I tried the "Baidu knows the answer" function, only to find that Baidu did not know the answer—of course, it wouldn't say, even if it knew. So then I tried Sina's "Sina loves questions" feature, only to find it didn't appreciate this particular inquiry. But by the end of it all I had a general picture of what had happened. It is actually all too typical a story, and to avoid causing this essay to provoke an allergic reaction I am going to withhold the names of all the people involved.

After a woman's sudden death, her family suspected she had been gang-raped. They demanded an autopsy, but the coroner's conclusion was that she had simply died of an illness. The family suspected the police of shielding the perpetrators and demanded a new autopsy, but they were stonewalled by the authorities. Hearing of this incident, three rights activists, concluding that the woman *had* been raped, circulated the news to chat rooms at home and abroad. The local public security held a news conference where they reiterated that the deceased died from natural causes, and soon after the people responsible for the posts were arrested by the local public security and the three netizens were sentenced to between one and two years in prison.

So that's basically the story. In terms of the case itself, the key issue is just how the victim died. Having no basis on which to make a judgment, I am in no position to side either with the rights activists or with the government. The government's view is that if they have made an announcement, then that constitutes proof. The rights activists view is that if they have looked into the case, then that constitutes proof. The questions I would raise are: In the countless disputes of this kind, is the government always in the wrong? Not necessarily. Are the rights activists always right? Not necessarily. But why is it that the government never fails to put itself in the worst possible light?

The local authorities so often have only themselves to blame for incidents like this becoming so fraught. If a person's death is truly caused by a sudden, catastrophic illness, then they should simply have a credible agency come and do the autopsy, and persuade the family to accept the findings. On the Internet many people are saying that the government urgently needs to set up a clean-government office so as to establish credibility. But I think that such a department is useless. If Hong Kong has very few cases of corruption, that's not because they have a "clean-government office," but because clean government is *independent*. I think that given China's national circumstances at the moment, it's not ready to have an independent body on the lines of a clean-government commission—if it were to be established and if it were to take its work seriously, then practically all officials and their relatives would be gone in an instant. The body that China most urgently needs is an independent coroner's office, one that enjoys independence and commands credibility, one that when necessary can broadcast its examinations live on television. If you think back over the mass protests that have taken place in China over the last few years, so many of them have been triggered by autopsies. The coroner's office is a key department in upholding social stability, because autopsies these days, no matter whether the results are genuine or faked, command no trust among the people. Although I suspect many autopsy findings are correct, the people are not wrong to be suspicious. A government that first decides the offense and then decides the crime is very likely to find that the people will master the same technique, so we must expect people to jump to the conclusion that their loved ones have been murdered, that the culprit is being shielded, and that the autopsy results have been fabricated. Because, in this society, if *you* aren't concerned about evidence, then neither am I, and if *you* are not transparent, then I'm going to indulge in speculation. And when I speculate, you say I'm engaging in slander, and when I press for an answer, you say this is a state secret, and when I make a big thing out of it, then you . . . then you . . . well, that makes it easy for you—that takes the matter out of your hands, for naturally the relevant authorities will notify the news oversight departments that this incident cannot be reported. However, what you're burying here is simply the seeds of hate.

Therefore, this incident could very easily have been resolved by the local authorities right from the start. If they had done an absolutely honest autopsy and verified that the victim had died of natural causes, then they could have persuaded the family; and if the autopsy had established that the victim had been murdered, then they could have arrested the culprit. Or, at the minimum, this issue could have been discussed openly, with everyone bringing forward their own evidence as part of the debate. But officialdom has always considered itself above that kind of procedure, for they think this would only lower their prestige. What's more, our officials always put themselves in a poor light as soon as they open their mouths: You simply never see them earnestly engaging in conversation using the kind of language that we human beings employ to communicate. They always revert to that robotic official jargon to resist ordinary people's appeals. Music aficionados will agree that tone is crucial, and when someone sings in a tone that you loathe, any song they sing is bound to be crap.

Now, how that girl died is no longer important—what matters is the verdict on those three rights activists. As for the crime of slander, it looks like prison terms are inevitable. Charges like this cannot be explained in legal terms—one needs to understand the outcome in terms of self-interest and established convention, because, to the government, face is so important. They've locked you up for all this time now—and on this pretext—and if you were now to be released, although the court may receive plaudits, how is public security going to manage in the future? They are all living in the same town and are bound to run into each other sooner or later, if not in the office then in the sauna, and how awkward that interaction would be. Actually, all these years, everyone has misunderstood the meaning of "the People's Court"—this doesn't mean a court that is of the people and for the people, what it means is a court that only makes itself responsible for resolving contradictions among the people, not between the people and government agencies.

Now that these three rights activists have been sentenced to a year or two in jail, many netizens think a dark age for the Internet is about to arrive, that rights activists are going to get brought in for retaliatory sanctions, that critical commentary posted on the Internet is going to be prohibited and punished, that freedom of speech is going to completely disappear. But given that we're dealing with law enforcement in a small county town, I think it's a mistake to attribute to these people such profound motives. When it comes down to it, this incident has only one meaning and conveys only one message, namely: See what we're capable of doing.

All right, you want to show us what you're capable of, and we've seen and we're afraid, but what we don't understand is—what is it *you're* so afraid of?

Yes, do come! Yes, do go!

_____

April 19, 2010

Recently reporters have been bombarding me with requests for interviews about the Shanghai Expo. This puts me in a difficult spot, because if I sing its praises my conscience won't rest easy, and if I find fault with it I won't be allowed to sleep easy. Since the expo is about to begin, I herewith provide answers to all the standard questions; please spare me any more inquiries.

What do you think the expo will bring to Shanghai and to China? What would you compare it to?

It's not a question, I think, of what the expo brings to China, but of what China brings to the expo. Because expos originally were never such big events, as information circulates more and more rapidly, the idea of the expo is increasingly outdated. It's China that has elevated the expo to a new level. If you really want an analogy, it's a bit like some international brand that's really popular in China — with all the hype it gets, when you are wearing one of those outfits you think you are occupying the pinnacle of fashion and enjoying the ultimate in luxury, but then when you ask about it abroad, you find that it's second string.

What do you think of the expo mascot—Haibao?

I think Haibao is a real pain. Setting aside the question of whether it's an attractive—or an original—design, the version of it we first saw was flat, and that has been the source of great difficulty for people trying to make it three-dimensional. Just what should his rear end look like? Does he have a tail? Does he have an ass? Does his ass have cleavage? This is very unclear. So when we look at the figures of Haibao that have been erected around the city, their front view is identical but the rear varies.

152

Once the expo is over, the pavilions will be removed—do you think this is a waste?

No, I don't think that's a waste at all. The original properties in that area had to be cleared in the first place, and then the government funded the construction of the China Pavilion—and helped other countries build their pavilions—so the government has been spending money all over the place. To keep these pavilions in Shanghai serves no purpose anyway—they can't serve as government office buildings, after all—so they may as well flatten the whole area and sell it off as real estate. That way, in the end, the expo isn't something run by the government or by business, but by mortgage slaves and real estate speculators.

If that's the case, why is the government going to preserve a handful of pavilions?

Well, of course they can't demolish them all—if they did that, they couldn't call it the "expo parcel" and sell it off at the highest price.

Some people are saying that while the expo is on, cars from other places have to wait in line for inspection on the way into Shanghai—often generating traffic jams several miles long that take hours to get through. Do you think there is a better way of handling this?

No, I can't help you there, because the government applies uniform security procedures whether they are on the lookout for thieves, terrorists, reactionary forces, or ordinary citizens. Although I have no way of knowing who exactly they are on the lookout for when they search every car and every person, I do know that if I was a bad guy I certainly wouldn't just stand there in line obediently, waiting to be searched with a bomb under my arm. The demarcation lines between cities are not as clearly defined as the borders between nations, and often a rice paddy is all that separates them, so if you set your mind to it it's not difficult at all to pass from one to another. I don't believe these security measures will really detect people who are determined to do something bad. But maybe the government thinks this makes a good deterrent, intimidating the bad guys so that they lose all courage. In that case, everyone just has to do their bit and wait in line.

In any case, I certainly support better security. So long as the government makes a reasonable appraisal of the pros and cons, I am willing to accept any kind of security procedure. Indirectly, in the name of the expo, a number of Shanghai residents have been killed or injured by construction vehicles, and I hope that no other lives will be threatened because of it.

How many visitors to Shanghai do you think the expo will bring in?

153

That's hard to say. One needs to make a distinction between people who make a trip to Shanghai specially to see the expo and those who go and have a look since they are visiting anyway. According to official sources, sixty million people will enter Shanghai during these six months. But Shanghai attracts a lot of visitors in any case, and by my reckoning, even without the expo, there would probably be fifty-nine million people visiting Shanghai for other reasons. When I go abroad for a holiday, whether a city is holding an expo does not have the slightest effect on my decision to visit it, but maybe foreigners are so innocent that they'll all be eager to come. Of course I have lots of friends who are looking forward to going to the expo, and I can understand that. The expo should be a really big scene, after all, and Chinese people have always loved to go to a fair—just think of all the people who turn up at a car show, for instance. Of course, I can also understand why so many Shanghai people are eagerly anticipating the opening of the expo, because if a lot of foreigners and out-of-towners are there, they can put on a nice demonstration for them of what an amazing city Shanghai is: house prices at fifty thousand yuan a square meter, parking spots at twenty yuan an hour, gasoline at more than a dollar a liter, all basic living expenses really high, the cost of living five times yours, and wages a fifth of yours, but we've not just survived—we're all ready to greet with open arms sightseers from all over the place. The Shanghai-nese have to be the most impressive exhibition objects in this city. I propose that some city residents be selected as art works and put on display in the China Pavilion.

How would you rate the city of Shanghai?

I was born here and will always love Shanghai and hope that it can be one of the world's most wonderful cities, even though my old neighborhood is now ruined by pollution. It's fair to say that if you have money, Shanghai is a great place: In terms of dining and shopping, entertainment and getting around, it's just fine. In more general economic terms, Shanghai is an adventurer's paradise, but hell for ordinary folks.

But Shanghai has no culture. If you go to a big city in another country, they'll tell you: We have such-and-such buildings, such-and-such hotels, such-and-such streets, such-and-such villas. . . . Administrators in Shanghai will proudly tell you: We have all that stuff, too. But when the others say: Here we have such-and-such writers, such-and-such directors, such-and-such artists, such-and-such exhibitions, such-and-such film festivals, our leaders go all quiet.

Why the lack of culture in Shanghai?

If you want real culture to develop, you need to loosen controls, and if you loosen controls that means allowing diverse voices to be heard, and if you allow diverse voices to be heard that's bound to raise the level of popular consciousness—and what a terrible thing that would be!

155

Officials tell us that on the one hand genetically engineered foods are harmless, but that on the other, these same foods are banned from the expo site, so that foreigners won't have to eat them. Isn't this a form of self-denigration?

What nonsense! This is an expression of confidence, confidence in the strong constitutions of us Chinese. Every day we breathe this air and drink this water, and we survive in all kinds of adverse conditions. Those foreigners would die after swallowing a single mouthful of weed-killer, but it takes three mouthfuls to kill us. So you're barking up the wrong tree.

Children, you're spoiling grandpa's fun

May 2, 2010

Now, children at a Taixing kindergarten have suffered a knife attack too.* Thirty-two of them have been injured; the death toll is still unclear. Because news of this incident followed so closely on the heels of the stabbings at a Nanping kindergarten, I thought at first that this all happened at the same facility.

In recent incidents where disturbed individuals have launched fatal attacks on others, the targets have all been either kindergartens or primary schools: This has clearly become a fashion among those who feel they have a score to settle with society, because in such places one will encounter the least resistance and be able to kill the greatest number of victims and cause the greatest amount of pain and fear—it is the most effective way of exacting revenge. With the exception of Yang Jia,† practically all these assailants have chosen

---

*In the spring and summer of 2010 a spate of attacks in Chinese schools and kindergartens caused the deaths of at least twenty-one children and adults and injured over ninety people.

†Yang Jia, an unemployed man in his late twenties, stabbed six Shanghai policemen to death in retaliation for alleged mistreatment after his arrest for riding an unlicensed bicycle. He was subsequently found guilty of murder and executed.

to target those weaker than themselves. This society has no pressure valves—killing the weakest has become the only way out. I propose that local government security guards be transferred to kindergartens, for a government that can't even keep children from harm doesn't deserve so much protection.

A major cause of these attacks is that this society is unjust and unfair. Yes, "to establish fairness and justice makes things brighter than sunlight itself." * But the sun doesn't come out every day. Don't you think maybe we have too many overcast days and dark nights? So, there's nothing so wonderful about suggesting that fairness and justice should be brighter than sunlight—the best thing would be to have sunshine all the time.

Concerning this incident in Taixing, there has been a clampdown on news coverage. Not only were these children born at the wrong time, it seems they died at the wrong time too. From the point of view of the powers that be, this incident is a distraction from all the festivities marking yesterday's opening of the Shanghai Expo. All we know is that there were thirty-two people injured; the hospital and the government keep repeating that there were no fatalities. But unofficially it is reported that a number of children died. So whom should we believe? Maybe we're inclined to believe the government, but then why is it that parents are prohibited from seeing their children? So far, the hospital and the media remain muzzled, with no pictures or video of the victims. And if a man goes on the rampage with a knife and manages to inflict wounds on thirty-two people but not one of them dies, one has to wonder: Was he trying to kill people, or perform medical procedures on them? He seems to have been way too careful. Maybe we're inclined to believe the rumors, but rumor is always prone to exaggeration, and without further documentation we cannot place credence in it, either. So I conducted an online search for "Taixing," and all it gave me was a

---

* Han Han is here quoting a remark made by Chinese premier Wen Jiabao at a press conference on March 14, 2010.

news report dated April 30: "In Taixing Three Happy Events Coincide."

What really surprises me is that the Taixing government, by muzzling the hospital and suppressing news and blocking the media and prohibiting visits and distracting attention and so forth, has so successfully converted everyone's anger with the assailant into anger with itself. This is quite unnecessary. You might think there is some special motive behind their secretiveness, but actually there isn't—apart from wanting to provide the ideal backdrop to the Shanghai Expo (and its paean to harmony), it's all just inertia, it's the government's ingrained habit when dealing with this kind of incident, the same old ritual in seven stages. Every time something happens when you're halfway through the feast, you:

conceal,
sequester,
expel,
ban,
spin,
compensate,
and cremate

—then back to the food and wine. Their way of handling issues is not much more refined than that of the slasher, and it's no wonder that one can now see posted on the Internet a couplet commemorating this incident:

Looking for the source of the grievance you want to vent?
Go out the door, turn left, and there's the government.

In just over a month, there have been five cases of killings in schools; in just one week, there have been two: on April 29 in Taixing, on April 30 in Weifang. I don't propose to examine here all the underlying social causes, all I want to say is: A man bursts into a kindergarten in Taixing and wounds thirty-two children, but this cannot be properly reported. If you add the kids' ages together, it comes to only a hundred years or so, but there's no place for their story in the papers, because a hundred miles away there's a big bash going on, where just the fireworks alone cost a hundred million yuan, and at the same time in their hometown they're getting ready for the International Tourism Festival, Commerce Talks, and Recreational Park Opening Ceremony, three happy occasions all at the same time.

Don't you see, children, you're spoiling grandpa's fun?

Poor children, it's you who are poisoned by the tainted milk powder, you who are harmed by the faulty vaccine, you who are crushed by the earthquake, you who are burned by the fire. Even if it's in the adults' world where things are going wrong, you're the ones on whom an adult seeks to exact vengeance. I hope it's true that, as the Taixing government claims, you are only injured and none of you have died. Your elders have failed in their duty, but I hope that when you grow up you can do better, not just protecting your own children but making society protect *all* its children.

Talking freely, wine in hand

May 7, 2010

Interviews with foreign media are different from those with domestic media, even if they sometimes ask the same questions and I give the same answers: What actually gets printed in the paper differs considerably. Foreign reporters' questions are relatively more direct—sometimes so direct as to be unanswerable, because if you were to ever answer them, my guess is that you'd only ever be speaking to foreign reporters from then on. If so, I tell them honestly, "I can't answer that question. It's not that I won't, it's that I can't. To answer that question would exact too high a price, one that's not worth paying—at least, not now. At the same time, I'm not willing to lie, so I'm just going to choose to keep my mouth shut. But you don't need to delete your question, for it's a good one. Just say that the interviewee dared not answer. Please excuse my weakness."

To be frank, I tend to be more expansive when responding to questions from Chinese reporters, because I know that however much I say and even if it's just me and the reporter having a chat, since the transcript undergoes the reporter's self-censorship there's nothing that will get into the paper that is not aboveboard. Faced with a foreign reporter, I will talk more in terms of my hopes for the future. An interview I just had with a Canadian journalist is a rather typical example, so here I'm going to quote some exchanges from it, with a few minor changes.

Q. Do you miss Google? If so, why? *

A. No, I don't miss Google at all. Google is like a girl who one day tells you out of the blue, "I'm leaving you."

"Oh no, darling, don't do that," you say. But she goes ahead and dumps you all the same.

Then you find, however, that you can actually have her whenever you want her. The only difference is that when you had her at your beck and call before, she would give you a carrot if that's what you asked for, and now when you say, "Where's the carrot?" she does a disappearing trick.

Q. If you had the chance to live abroad—in Canada, for instance—would you make the move? Why or why not?

A. If it was just a short-term arrangement, for a holiday or a race or business, that's something I'd be happy to do, but I am not interested in settling abroad permanently. Canada is a beautiful country with a comfortable lifestyle, a good ecological balance, and a high per capita GDP. My country has a high GDP but low per capita GDP, severe pollution, and corrupt officials, and sometimes it takes one step forward and two steps back, but I fully intend to remain where I am, watching my country progress or helping it along a bit—it is my homeland, after all. Another reason is that in my native land it's natural enough to be surrounded by corrupt Chinese officials, but if I move to another country only to discover that

---

* In early 2010, Google was engaged in a dispute with the Chinese government; in March 2010 it decided to redirect searches on its Chinese website to its site in Hong Kong.

I'm still rubbing shoulders with corrupt Chinese officials, that will really push me over the edge.*

Q. How should other countries, including Canada, view China's growing strength and its more prominent role in international affairs?

A. That's really a question you should ask our officials and our leaders. But what I can tell you is this: all you need to do is have a look at how they responded to that kind of question when other people asked it, and you've already got your answer. To find out their position on other issues of interest to you, just follow the same procedure.

Q. How do you account for China's hypersensitivity?

A. That's very hard to do. All I can say is this: Only an independent judiciary can be a true judiciary. But in our country, the judiciary cannot be independent, because that would be out of line with our national circumstances. What does "national circumstances" mean? They mean that making money is all that matters. What's the best guarantee of being able to make money? Power. Judicial independence will limit power. If you limit power, how are those people with power—and their families—going to be able to make so much money? So you see, judicial independence isn't the right fit for China.

Q. What kind of country would you like to see China become? (This question came from a Japanese reporter.)

A. A country that doesn't resort to land sales and real estate and low-end assembly production to achieve high GDP—and high per capita GDP. A country where good people don't

163

---

* Chinese officials seeking a foreign haven where they can enjoy their ill-gotten gains have found Canadian cities such as Toronto and Vancouver attractive choices.

have to jump over the wall and where bad people end up in jail.* A country whose culture has an impact on the world, whose literature and art other nations imitate. A country that has as clean an environment and as free an atmosphere as other places, where you can enjoy the spectacle of seeing power confined inside a cage, where you can talk freely, wine in hand, and say everything that's on your mind.

* To "jump over the wall" is to circumvent China's Internet censorship (sometimes referred to as the Great Firewall of China) by resorting to proxy servers that are not subject to government restrictions.

Those scallions that
just won't wash clean

May 14, 2010

Recently, Fujian Province has come up with ten principles for institutions of higher education. The most eye-catching of them is No. 2: "Those who in the course of educational work circulate erroneous views that violate the Communist Party's line, strategy, or policies, or the Party's basic theory, or the state's laws and decrees, and who create an adverse environment for instilling in students correct ideals, beliefs, and political allegiance, will be subject to veto power and dismissed from their appointments."

What's comforting is that as I was reading the first part of this long sentence, I was anticipating that it would culminate with the words "will be shot," but actually it is just a case of being "voted out" of office, so this counts as a big improvement over the days of Mao Zedong. As for who has the power to cast this vote, that is not an interesting question—what concerns me is that it's next to impossible to grasp this "line," "strategy," and "theory," for although those in power expect us to have unified thought, they themselves are often unable to do so. I seem to recall that there was a discussion about the tripartite division of powers in my high school curriculum, and both my politics textbook and my politics teacher said at the time that the division of powers is a good thing, but these days I keep reading official articles and speeches which insist that the division of powers is an erroneous concept. You know that I am someone with only a middle school diploma, and I dropped out of school before I could take my studies of politics any further, but I just feel perturbed—I feel anxious about the fate of those politics instructors and textbook editors who have disseminated erroneous thought. All along they have been regurgitating materials that the leaders gave them, only to find that if they handle things improperly they will be disciplined by the leaders, because those scripts reflect the way the leaders thought last night and this morning the leaders had a different idea when they got out of bed.

166   I saw somewhere a neat description of that phenomenon, and the gist of it was: A man gets into his car and immediately activates the right-turn indicator, drives forward a few yards, only to turn left. That wouldn't be so bad, but then he makes a complete U-turn. So, if you're run over by this kind of driver, you can only curse your bad luck.

When a journalist ferrets out the truth, when a history teacher lectures on the patterns of the past, when a writer presents things honestly, when a film director depicts real life, at best they will have committed an ideological error and at worst they will have perpetrated a crime. And when someone offends in this fashion, others will indulge in speculation: He has been "invited out for a coffee," he has been banned, he has been arrested, when actually in the end he may not get into so much trouble and all that may happen is that the evidence of his crime is purged from view, but people still don't feel relaxed—rather, they feel all the more anxious on their own account, suspecting that it's only because the guy is quite famous that the government has hesitated to take action—maybe the government won't have any scruples about taking action against me?

It has to have taken a lot of reinforcement to build up that level of instinctive anxiety.

In any era, even when brainwashing becomes as routine as washing vegetables, there are bound to be a few scallions that don't get rinsed clean. In the old days people would have hacked away and discarded those dirty leaves, but with the changing of the guard these unclean scallions are asked simply to keep to themselves as they grow. However, if they try to share their thoughts with the other onions, they will be immediately be squashed flat by the ones who insist on playing dumb.

Many people think that the subtext of the Fujian initiative is that recently some history teachers and university professors have been a bit too vocal, and of course I've seen in today's news that the history teacher Yuan Tengfei has been investigated—along with the Heaven on Earth Night Club—but I doubt that the two things are linked. When the Sensitive Council has not yet shown its hand, the government is not going to respond so rapidly nor are the various departments going to coordinate so seamlessly. It's just a co-incidence, a routine decree from an educational department. Some kind of decree like this governs all professions in China—it's simply that the precise language may take different forms. In the same way, all raffles share a common principle: The authority to interpret the rules rests with the sponsoring body. And I don't propose to discuss the question of who has the power to decide whether someone else's thought is correct or incorrect, for that topic is meaningless, since the answer is obvious. Who has the power? It's the people in power, of course, who have that power. Everything that bolsters their interests and their power is, of course, correct, and everything not conducive to promoting their interests and enhancing their power is naturally incorrect. As soon as you have grasped that principle, you'll never have to tie yourself into knots wondering what is right and what is wrong.

As for you history teachers, literature teachers, and politics teach-ers, what kind of role do you think you will play and what kind of verdict do you think will be passed on you in the textbooks of the future? Perhaps you are simply a vegetable that is not in charge of its own affairs, but your students are your seedlings. Try to be real teachers, imparting to your students common sense and reflection, independence and a sense of justice, so that in your old age, when you tell your grandchildren you once served in this profession, you will feel a surge of pride rather than be stricken with shame.

Youth

May 28, 2010

A high school friend of mine had no great aspirations, but was healthy and eager to work. After a long search, he landed a job in an assembly plant, for a salary of one thousand five hundred yuan a month. Often he would work overtime, which sometimes was paid and sometimes was not, for a total of two thousand yuan a month. He lived six or seven miles away from his workplace, so he bought a scooter, leaving home early and coming home late. Recently married, he couldn't afford to buy a house. Fortunately, his parents did have some rental income: Like other families in his home village, they built a three-story house and rented out the first and second floor to migrant laborers — six rooms at two hundred fifty yuan rent each, bringing in an extra monthly income of one thousand five hundred yuan. Those out-of-towners typically lived as a family, three to a room, each of them earning a bit over eight hundred yuan a month, walking or cycling to local factories. These factories, set up by investors from elsewhere, manufactured chemical products and polluted more heavily than the assembly plants. Most of them have now closed down. The few that remain are able to turn a slight profit, but if they were to clean up their act and reduce emissions, that would put them in the red, and if that happened they wouldn't be able to pay taxes and make a contribution to GDP, so the local government can't afford to enforce regulations.

My friend feels he's not done so badly—he's found a wife, anyway—but pretty much all his income is spent just on basic subsistence and any major purchase is out of the question. He doesn't dare change his job or head off to some other region to try his luck, in part because there is no social safety net, and if by chance something happened and he missed out on a month's wages, there would just be no way to carry on. Looking ahead to the birth of a child, he and his wife would like to buy a house in the town and acquire an urban residence permit, but an apartment in one of the satellite towns near Shanghai costs at least half a million yuan. For that, he would need to work without eating and drinking for twenty-five years, and what he'll get for that is just the basic shell of an apartment—he'd need to go hungry for another five years to get it properly fixed up.

His next-door neighbor, another friend of mine, has just graduated from university and gets paid a bit more. But his girlfriend has higher expectations: She won't marry him until he has a house in the city. An older city apartment costs at least two million yuan, so my friend needs to work for sixty years—or his family needs to rent out their house to eight migrant-worker families for a hundred years—before he can afford to buy it. So all they can hope for is forced relocation. Even if the government purchases their house for half a million and then sells off the land for five million, they're not going to protest, for the half million can cover the down payment on an apartment in the city. How they manage in the future remains to be seen, but at least this way he would be able to marry. As for where his parents will live after the house is demolished, that's certainly an issue, but maybe they'd be able to rent a reasonably sized room in another local's house for three hundred yuan or so, as an interim arrangement.

My first friend's previous job involved rotating shifts and the factory was far from his home; he developed health problems and resigned the job to take his current position, hoping for less overtime and higher pay; his employer indicated he would get a raise of one hundred yuan this year and another one hundred yuan next year. Last week he told me that his father is probably going to get a job abroad as a bricklayer: If he works abroad for three years, he should make two hundred thousand yuan. I asked him what his plan was, and he said he'd just carry on as he was doing—what other choice is there? His mother is screwing in light bulbs for eight hundred yuan a month. This young man in his twenties is looking at his own future thirty years from now: a father in his fifties who has to go abroad to work for two years. This family in the outskirts of Shanghai dislikes the migrant laborers, for they compete for jobs in the local factories and have driven down salaries to just a few hundred yuan a month, and the ratio of outsiders to locals in the areas is now over ten to one. At the same time, they have no choice but to depend on them, because they pay over ten thousand yuan in rent each year.

Such is the life of ordinary folk in the outskirts of Shanghai, and this family might actually be doing pretty well. It's situations like this that have led so many employees at Foxconn to throw themselves off buildings: repetitive work, very low wages, a hopeless future.* But if they go somewhere else, wages will be even lower. The cost of living is high: Though they won't go hungry or suffer cold, there's nothing else they can do. And giving them enough to eat is presented by the government as a huge achievement, a notable contribution to the world and to humanity. How the authorities wish they could get their hands on the archives of prehistory or photographs of the Ice Age, for that would really show what a big debt the people owe to

* Foxconn, a large electronics business headquartered in Taiwan, operates extensive manufacturing facilities in mainland China where both the iPhone and iPad are produced. Foxconn has often been accused of abusive employment practices, and over a dozen of its Chinese workers committed suicide in 2010.

the government! Since just having enough to eat is such an accomplishment, how could people possibly have higher goals than that? Although my friend is under a lot of pressure, at least his friends and family are close by. But for the vast majority of young migrant workers, their families are a thousand miles away or more, and their families may well not treat them with much affection, for how much you earn is commonly the sole criterion Chinese families have for determining the value of a child.

These young workers represent a sector of society unfamiliar to most Internet users. It's rare to find chat rooms where current employees of Foxconn tell stories about the suicides of their coworkers or talk about their own lives, for they don't have time to do those things and may not even know how. The garish, self-indulgent life outside has nothing to do with them, and they have no hopes of love, either, given the reality of their existence. Maybe only when they throw themselves off the roof does the value of their lives find some expression, when their having once existed is briefly mentioned and remembered, although now they have become only a statistic.

Psychological counseling is useless. When they see our women cuddling the rich, and the rich cuddling the officials, and the officials cuddling the bosses, and the bosses cuddling Lin Chi-ling,* how are you going to give them psychological counseling? If I make inquiries, I find that my former classmates are all struggling. If there are men who are doing okay, it's because they depend on their parents, and if there are women who are doing okay, it's because they have married well. Everyone envies your benefits at Foxconn: wages issued on time, accommodation provided, and overtime with pay. You tell people you're a robot, but those people say they're just a pile of shit. In an area of several hundred square kilometers, there's not a single realistic rags-to-riches story to tell: Such is the life of so many Chinese youth.

---

* A Taiwanese supermodel.

If the Foxconn workers were paid ten times what they are now, would the suicides stop? So long as inflation isn't ten times what it is now, then yes—the suicides would cease. Of course, their employer would never raise their pay that much—and if they did, the government would issue an edict forbidding it. Why have our politicians been able to pump up their chests on the world political stage and make some political moves and play some political tricks? It's because of you, China's cheap labor: you are China's gambling chips, hostages to GDP. Whether it is socialism with Chinese characteristics or capitalism with feudal characteristics, in the next ten years there is no way out for these young people. This is so sad: warm blood that should be coursing through veins—spilled on the ground, instead.

Orphan of Asia

———————

June 24, 2010

Orphan of Asia was originally the title of a 1945 novel by the Taiwanese author Wu Zhuoliu, written during the Japanese occupation; the book describes the tragic predicament of a Taiwanese intellectual who is mistreated by the Japanese but also discriminated against in China. Later, the name was applied to a detachment of the Chinese Nationalist Army stranded in the border area of southwest China; their story formed the basis for a Hong Kong feature film. Luo Dayou wrote a song for that movie, which was set in the region of Yunnan, Burma, and Laos, although he was no doubt also thinking of Taiwan's isolation at the time. One of those places is now one of Asia's problem children, but the others are among Asia's promising youngsters; the true orphan of Asia is North Korea.

Last week I watched Brazil play North Korea in the World Cup, a match I had been looking forward to for a long time, in part because I like South American soccer, in part because North Korea is just so mysterious. "Do you think the Korean players will be shot when they get home," I joked with my friends, "because they have had a chance to see the world?" After watching the first half, another thought occurred to me. "North Korea actually has always been good enough to reach the finals," I said, "it's just that the past few World Cup finals have been held in developed countries, so it wasn't convenient for them to progress beyond the qualifying round. This time the finals are in South Africa, where there's a huge gap between rich and poor, so the North Korean government took their team and dumped them in a South African shanty town and said, 'See, this is how you live when you don't have socialism.' Generalissimo Kim Jung-il had decided it was all right for them to take part."

In this first match the North Korean team played stylish soccer and were very sportsmanlike as well: No playacting or pushing and shoving, and if they fell down they were back on their feet right away. Whether out of sympathy for the underdog or out of solidarity with other Asians, I was touched by their performance. And when they finally scored a goal, I was delighted—although I did remind my friends that just because they like the Korean players and the Korean people they shouldn't take things any further and start liking Kim Jung-il and the dominant ideology there. When it came to the second match, many people quite fancied North Korea's chances, thinking they might well upset Portugal. But experience tells us that with this kind of country, whatever the setting, once things start to go wrong the whole place is likely to fall apart. When North Korea was thrashed 7–0, my friends began to worry once more about the fate of the team when they got back home.

As a neighbor of ours, North Korea has always been a pain in the neck. A lot of people take the simplistic view that North Korea is bound to be our friend forever, since our two states pledge allegiance to the same belief system, but this is a strange way of looking at things—a bit like saying that just because we're both Argentina fans, then we have to be friends too. Of course, in the end everyone's realized we're actually fake Argentina fans, but fake in different ways. Others take the naïve view that if there's another war

176

we will have to come to North Korea's aid, because we can't have a capitalist country right there on our doorstep and because we made huge sacrifices to defend North Korea the first time round. That's an odd position to take, too, for who can say that two bosom pals will never have a falling out, and there's no guarantee that the North Korean people really thank us for what we did, in any case. And if war did break out between North and South Korea, the North might well lob a few nuclear warheads at the South but end up getting beaten anyway, and the following might happen: With South Korean territory affected by nuclear radiation, the two sides might switch ends—just like halfway through a soccer match—and we'd have South Korea on the north side of the thirty-eighth parallel for a change. Actually, it's not important what ideology is supported by the countries adjacent to us, for that's not a major issue in contemporary warfare—what matters is whether our neighbors are civilized, and whether we are.

North Korea has abundant natural resources, a population proportionate to the country's size, and a commendable national spirit; for it to be reduced to its current level of poverty has to count as quite an achievement. Some people attribute North Korea's problems to the sanctions imposed by the international community, particularly the United States, but I'm not sure they truly understand the country. Of course, I can't claim to truly understand the country either, but in an age when information is so widely available, if a country is so difficult to get to know and if its citizens have even more difficulty getting to know the rest of the world—or risk being shot if they try—then it is bound to be poor. The less access to information, the more backward the economy—that is inevitable. What's ironic is that this extremely autocratic nation that does everything it can to brainwash its people calls itself the "Democratic People's Republic of Korea," just as the bloody and dictatorial red regime in Cambodia in the 1970s, which in just four years caused the death of a fifth of its population, called itself "Democratic Kampuchea."

It's only when they recite the complete name of their country, I bet, that the people of North Korea ever have the chance to mention the word *democracy*.

We can't interfere in other countries' internal politics and we can't comment on our own—all we can do is comment on the former. Like a straggler looking back sympathetically at someone trailing even further behind, I always keep hoping that North Korea can join the world, can stop being Asia's orphan, even if it doesn't do any better than us. Here in China we're always ambivalent about how far to go: heading right, then veering left; one hand waving, one hand clenched; pressing forward, then pushing back; steering west and talking east; but at least we're part of the world, at least we're never again going to perform a loyalty dance, tears welling up in our eyes as we fondle the leader's portrait. For everyone to submit to the authority of one person or one view can never be the standard by which one determines the success of a state or a regime. Actually, when we look at it now, all that fuss we used to make about this class or that, about the correct outlook and the right banner, it was all just a game or all just a dream. Forty or fifty years ago, we were always getting in a tizzy about which class was going to have power, but in fact that's not the issue at all, for any group of people who get power will inevitably become a new class—there is no evidence to show they will naturally and inevitably uphold the interests of the class to which they originally belonged. No matter what class you identify with, no matter what kind of thinker you are, or politician, or military strategist, working out how to get power is not such a towering achievement—it's the one who works out how to *limit* power who is truly great.

Finally I'd like to share with you that song of Luo Dayou's—one I've always liked—as a way of expressing our hope that the people of North Korea can live better lives or at least not starve, and also to remind ourselves that once you're lost in the bitter sea, it's so hard to get out of it.

The orphan of Asia weeps in the wind
Red mud on sallow chin
White terror in brown eyes
West wind wails in eastern skies
Nobody plays straight, my boy
Everyone wants your favorite toy
So much searching up and down
For answers that just can't be found
So many sighs of despair at night
So many tears just out of view
Mother dear, how can this be right
Mother dear, how can this be true

Protect the—[unacceptable input]

September 12, 2010

Some friends have asked me why I'm not taking a stand on the Diaoyu Islands incident and condemning Japan.* What I tell them is: Even though none of the earth under my feet is my own, I still pay a lot of attention to issues about territory. When I first heard about this business, I dashed off a comment online with great conviction: "Protect the Diaoyu Islands!" But the result was that the chat room host told me I was trying to publish illegal content and asked me to revise what I'd written. I racked my brains to think of another way to put it, and it was only when I altered the post to read "Protect the Senkaku Islands" that it could be published without further ado.

This latest contretemps is truly a major incident, one that has

---

* The small, uninhabited Diaoyu Islands, known in Japan as the Senkaku Islands, lie in the East China Sea between Taiwan and Okinawa, and are claimed both by China and Japan. On September 10, 2010, a Chinese fishing boat collided near the islands with patrol boats from the Japanese Coast Guard, who then took the fishing boat and its crew into custody. China submitted a strong protest and demanded the fishermen's immediate release. Japan soon permitted the crewmen to return home, but held the captain until September 24.

compelled the Ministry of Foreign Affairs to work through the weekend on formulating a protest statement. If you're enjoying a perfect life, with wife and child, house and car, work and leisure, health and fitness all in perfect shape, then, if you're appropriately stirred by patriotic sentiment and in no mood to "conceal your strength and bide your time," then of course you should feel free to protect the Diaoyu Islands. But if there are things in your life not quite so secure, my feeling is that you should attend to them first, rather than worrying about something so remote.

But perhaps you will say to me, "When the big issues are so clear-cut, what do one's own personal little losses amount to?" That's true, but people have the right to define for themselves what the big issues are. In this case, for example, I think first we have to look at the government's attitude—how can you rush ahead of the leadership? If the leadership denounces Japan's actions, that means they want you to condemn them too, but if they simply express regret, that means you can put a stop to your denunciations. If the leadership wants denunciation and you want to take action, that reaches the limit of what the leadership can tolerate, and if you really take action the leadership will have to punish you, because the leadership is playing a game of chess with a lot of pieces and since you're just a single piece, how have you got the right to jump right off the board? And on this board you are a black piece, whereas the leadership is a white one, in part because the working people are bound to be a bit darker-skinned. Black is the color that suits you best, but the most important thing is, the leadership that is already washed white wants you to sing blackface when you charge forward, whereas at the key moment they will sing whiteface.* If you're unlucky you'll find out later that the leadership has happily struck a business deal with the supposed aggressors.

Regarding the Diaoyu Islands issue, I am sure that our govern-

---

* In Peking opera, actors wearing blackface paint tend to play honest, brave, impetuous characters, whereas those in whiteface play crafty, calculating roles.

ment's primary concern is its firm control over the domestic situation; whether there is oil under the sea is not so much what's on their minds. Oil is what the Japanese want, and that's why they suddenly got so interested in the islands in the 1970s. But the Chinese government only cares about stability—they don't want any unpredictable risks in foreign relations or military affairs, and so this has caused an issue which isn't actually all that complicated to be dragged out interminably. There may well be another area on our borders that is similarly controversial and capable of provoking friction and local hostilities with neighboring countries, but just as long as it's not very big and its loss would not affect China's chicken-like shape and it's located in some out-of-the-way corner that the people and the media don't know much about, the government may well feel that it's best to be somewhat accommodating and treat it as though it's already been sold off to a real estate mogul, since neither rooster nor hen are all that bothered about it. But the Diaoyu Islands have often been in the news these last few decades, so public attention is high, particularly after all those scenes on TV of our leaders receiving foreign dignitaries at the Diaoyutai State Guesthouse. It would be just too embarrassing if after all this fuss Diaoyutai ends up in someone else's hands, and so pressing the claim for the Diaoyu Islands has become a matter of pride for the government, and I'm confident they won't be ceded to another country any time soon. But for the Chinese government, the best solution is to keep on dragging things out, delaying things until there's another shift in the tectonic plate, so that the Diaoyu Islands directly get tacked onto Fujian Province, for that will make things a lot simpler, and we can sort out questions of underwater petroleum some other time. So I'm not worried that the Diaoyu Islands will be occupied by the Japanese, even though in fact they've already pretty much done that. And in terms of this current incident, the best outcome is that the captain is held for ten days, and after nine days of us strongly condemning and gravely protesting, the Japanese let the guy go, for that way finally our protests have borne fruit. As for the people who sing blackface, of course it does no harm to sing when they've got nothing better to do with their time, so long as they don't get into it too deeply and don't let it affect their lives, for don't forget that it's even more important to protect the things that you and your family should have, and don't get upset if you find that you've already drained your cup and the leadership hasn't even opened its bottle, and don't imagine that you're really responding to the nation's greatest emergency, for the nation has a lot more pressing issues than this.

Should we or shouldn't we?

September 19, 2010

Yesterday, September 18—a sensitive date in China*—some of my friends debated whether or not to take to the streets, since it seems there is no objection to us demonstrating against Japan, for the Diaoyu Islands, and for our fishing-boat captain. Finally, in a nation where in many chat rooms it's impossible even to type the word *demonstrate*, we are free to demonstrate. So should we or should we not take part in a demo on this subject?

First of all, I think it's true to say we have three classes in Chinese society today: masters, slaves, and dogs. But often a person may take on double roles. As for which two roles these are, I doubt that anyone is going to feel that he's playing the master. Not long ago, the masters needed slaves to echo their words and wait on them hand and foot, but now they need dogs to do some barking, and according to dog logic, no matter how it's treated by its master, it always has to protect the property whenever an outsider encroaches.

---

* September 18, 1931, was the date of the Mukden Incident, when Japanese forces invaded Manchuria on the pretext that Chinese subversives had committed an act of sabotage.

Keeping this point in mind helps us to think more clearly about the question. But the good thing is: We also have one more choice, simply to remain spectators. Why would we choose to do that? In the eyes of the powers that be, the difference between a little thing and a big thing is simply that the first may provoke one protest and the second may provoke eleven; the site of real privilege and authority has not exerted itself in any way; apart from calling in the Japanese ambassador multiple times, our diplomats are quite composed; and we don't see any real determination on the part of our government to take retaliatory measures—no economic sanctions, never mind a show of military force. They're hiding their strength and biding their time, so we might as well just do the same. After all, it's enough that we are dogs—why reduce ourselves to the role of dogs that perform tricks to order?

If we take a good look at how things have developed, it seems that our leaders are not really that indignant—they just feel useless, so naturally we feel useless along with them. How would it make sense to take to the streets to show how useless you feel—doesn't that show you're even more of a no-hoper? When the leaders lose face, we try to give them a boost, but when they *have* face they slap us down. When I am abused, I can't protest, but when you are abused you want me to protest—isn't that humiliating?

"Well," you say, "this incident involves our whole nation, our national territory—it's a case of us all being bullied. Even if the government doesn't act, your life is in such a mess that you've got nothing to lose, so why not put yourself in the front line?" Yes, I could do that, but my strong opinion is that it's the government's job to do something, and that's a lot more important than us protesting against the Japanese, because territorial issues have never been things that the people at large can solve or should try to resolve— particularly in our country, where ordinary people don't even own an inch of land, where all land is leased from the government. For me, what this issue amounts to in the end is my landlord wrangling with someone else about a fallen tile. The tile fell off the landlord's roof in a gale, but the landlord doesn't dare pick it up, because that might lead to a fight with the neighbor. So why would we tenants want to get mixed up in this? People who've got no land to their name go to fight for someone else's land, people stripped of dignity fight to defend someone else's dignity—just how low can you fall?

But it is true that a demonstration on this occasion would be safe, fun, and cool, and the biggest thing in its favor is that after the demo is over you can still work and study normally and you may even get credit for it in the future, so it does no harm for university students and ordinary people to join in—it gives them the chance to try something new and sing blackface. If the government sings whiteface, maybe it will have some effect. What's more, there's a difference between those who join in a demonstration now and those who did so before: In the past there was no distinction between nation and government, and protestors could be sold out by the authorities without it ever occurring to them that they should object, whereas now many young people are capable of understanding more fully what this whole patriotism business is about, and although they are still indignant they have begun to reflect on the causes of their uselessness and passivity, and looking back they can consider more objectively the relationship between the nation and the government, so this is some kind of progress. In any society, the nation is like a woman and the party in power is like a man who possesses her. There are happy, ideal partnerships, there are harmonious relationships, and there are cases of domestic violence and tense relations; there are women who divorce and remarry and others who are never given the chance to remarry, but however it works out, when you love a woman you can't love her man at the same time.

In the end, none of these things matter. What matters is if today I can demonstrate in support of Tang Fuzhen and Xie Chaoping,*

* Tang Fuzhen, a resident of Chengdu, died on November 13, 2009, after setting herself on fire in protest at the forced demolition of her home. Xie Chaoping, an investigative journalist, was arrested on August 23, 2010, after the publication of his book *The Great Relocation*, an exposé of the disastrous aftermath following construction of a Mao-era dam across the Yellow River.

then tomorrow I will certainly feel a lot more like taking to the streets in support of the Diaoyu Islands and the Olympic torch. But there's something wrong with that argument: If you actually can demonstrate in support of Tang Fuzhen and Xie Chaoping, it's highly unlikely that there will be issues with the Diaoyu Islands and the Olympic torch and it's even less likely that the Tang and Xie incidents would take place in the first place. When a people cannot demonstrate peacefully in response to a domestic problem, any protest they make about something external has no more meaning than a dance extravaganza.

Do we need the truth,
or just the truth that fits our needs?

January 2, 2011

It's been a week since Village Chief Qian's tragic death.* Yesterday marked the seventh day of Buddhist mourning, and the uproar has still not subsided. I read up on the story as soon as I could, and like everyone else I was outraged by the Leqing police spokesman's dismissive remark, "There's no logical explanation for why he died in such unusual circumstances." But I have let days pass without writing anything about this, because I am not sure what actually happened. A week ago I was chatting with some friends online and one of them said, "It's really terrible! In Wenzhou somebody was held down on the ground by four security officers, and then a construction vehicle came and ran him over, crushing him to death." The friend said all this in a very confident tone, as though fully in

---

* Qian Yunhui, a village chief who had protested against abuses by the local government, died on December 25, 2010, after being hit and crushed by a truck. According to some reports, he had been forcibly pinned to the ground by security men so that the truck would run over him.

command of the facts. At the time I didn't know the story of how this whole thing unraveled and responded offhandedly with the comment, "Why did they have to hire four security guards to hold him down? The more people involved, the easier for the facts to emerge." Only after I got back home did I find out more. Although there were still some questions in my mind, I too was inclined to believe that Chief Qian had been murdered, or at least that there had been some monkey business. But still I hesitated to comment, because I knew that this was simply the story that I needed to hear, and that there was a chance it wasn't quite what had happened.

My family is from a village on the outskirts of Shanghai, an area where large swathes of land are often appropriated at rock-bottom prices, with compensation set at just a few hundred yuan per square meter. Former farmland is sold off at a huge profit to chemical plants and severe pollution ensues. In the face of a river full of dead fish, the National Environmental Monitoring Center can declare that the water quality is normal, and as to why the fish have died, their conclusion is much the same as that of the Leqing police: There's no logical explanation. Later, my home village planned Asia's biggest logistics port, Asia's biggest sculpture garden, and Asia's biggest electronics emporium, but none of these projects actually has reached fruition and all that we are left with is Asia's most poisonous chemical industry. Resenting all those land sales by the government as I do, I have a great admiration for Chief Qian. The story as we would like to hear it goes like this: An honest old village chief, engaged for years in a struggle with the local forces of evil, has been jailed multiple times for defending people's rights, and now he has been murdered by the government—or by a loose alliance of officials and businessmen—and his death has been falsely presented as a simple traffic accident. The villagers, realizing what happened, demanded that the culprits be punished, but they have been ruthlessly suppressed by riot police. The police seized many legitimate protesters and relatives of Chief Qian, carried off the body, used coercion or bribery to silence people in the know, muzzled the media, making this an appalling miscarriage of justice.

But the question is: Is that really what happened? I know that this is a truth you and I are very happy to accept, one that we hope to see established, one that validates the burning indignation we feel about the injustices that often take place in this part of the earth. What is the real truth, I do not know, because the government often lies and, no matter whether something is true or false, always handles issues as though struggling with a guilty conscience, so I cannot entirely believe the official explanation. But nor do I trust many Internet commentators' conjectures, because I don't believe you can reach a reliable verdict just by looking at a photograph, nor do I believe that just by watching a couple of episodes of Lie to Me you can make a judgment about whether someone is lying or not. As for the so-called suspicious points that people came out with later, they are becoming more and more contrived, like the claim that a construction vehicle cannot possibly have covered a certain distance at a certain speed—this shows some people have got so emotional they've taken leave of their senses.

191

A bit later, some citizens' investigation teams, including a number of lawyers, went to Leqing to look into things. Everyone naturally expected that they would not only refute the police's story and find evidence of murder but also expose an even more sinister plot, but to everyone's surprise the result of their investigation was basically the same as that of the police. If that is the truth, it's a truth that a lot of people don't need, so these investigation teams naturally aroused suspicion, becoming in the eyes of skeptics nothing more than a tour group in the pocket of the government—perhaps specifically sent to the area to soothe and placate those angry commentators. Although the process of the investigation was somewhat rushed and the evidence reviewed was incomplete, I personally have confidence in the lawyers' and journalists' integrity, and I'm not convinced that the government would be able to buy or train these individuals, who are not normally susceptible to pressure. Nor do I believe that the government would engage in an elaborate masquerade by sending out a citizens' investigation team to pull wool over the eyes of the people, because officials lack this degree of intelligence and resourcefulness—if the government was so meticulous in its efforts to deceive, we wouldn't see so many incidents handled so disastrously and there wouldn't be such an adversarial relationship between the government and the people. The government should take advantage of this period when our naïve citizens still imagine they might get somewhere by going to Beijing to bring grievances before the central authorities to give some thought to these questions: Why do so many people not believe what you say? Why do so many people think that to murder someone who is constantly petitioning for redress is something that you are capable of doing? Why is it that people with credibility immediately become scoundrels when the result of their investigation is the same as yours? Why is it that your way of hushing things up only succeeds in drawing attention to them more? No matter whether he was murdered or whether he died in an accident, Chief Qian should rest easy in his grave, because this incident has made everyone aware of the inequity that villagers suffer and aware that the credibility of his enemies is so very weak.

Sometimes the truth does not correspond to the people's needs, but the truth matters more than sentiment, and sentiment matters more than standpoint. I don't think we should just take it for granted that things are a certain way and then criticize people on that assumption—after all, that's the all-too-familiar package the government has been trying to ram down our throats for years.

On begging

February 10, 2011

My car sometimes makes an incredible rattle, and friends ask me if the exhaust pipe is loose. "No," I say, "it's money shaking around." I usually put a bunch of one-yuan coins in the car, so that I have something to give beggars who accost me at traffic lights or in a parking lot.

I have mixed feelings about beggars. On the one hand, I know a lot of them are just pretending to be penniless, because the streets are empty when I tend to go out at night and more than once I have seen beggars being picked up in cars. On the other hand, whether genuine or fake, some of them seem really pathetic, so I tend to dole out a few coins if I run into one. But over time I have become rather numb to it all, and these days my charity is more a habit than a true act of compassion. Chinese beggars are always looking for a handout when you're out and about, and most of them are children. Sometimes they will stick to you like a limpet, especially if you're with a girl. If you don't cough up, you come across as self-important and hard-hearted. If you do give money, you find yourself with a whole cluster of kids around you and no amount of coins will be enough to go round. If you give out a large sum, it looks as though you're putting on a show, and most of the time you know you're simply abetting evil. Once I gave a twenty-yuan note to one of several children surrounding me and said, "Here, share this with your pals—I don't have any change." He looked at me and dashed off like a puff of smoke. In a second the other children were all over me, and I found myself with a boy and a girl clutching each of my legs and really understood the idea of "children at the knee." That being said, beggars do help me appreciate the rate of inflation, for if you offer a panhandler one yuan today, this elicits a very different reaction from that of a few years ago.

After that, I asked someone why so many children are begging, and was told that it's a form of business. I'm happy, at least, that most of the beggars I have encountered have no physical deformities. Recently I learned from online commentators that some kidnapped children are deliberately maimed so that they can beg for money more effectively, which made me think of the crippled children I used to see sprawled on wooden carts and it made me wonder if they, too, had been victimized like that. It is illegal to force children to beg, and Public Security has asked people to call the police immediately if they see children being made to beg. The problem is: Although I have had plenty of experience with panhandlers, I have never once witnessed an adult forcing a child to beg. So I think that any form of begging by children should be prohibited, whether it is their parents or others who put them up to it. And such a ban should not be hard to enforce, because begging tends to take place at busy intersections, where there should be an adequate number of police on duty. Once we have such a law in place, I'm sure people will have enough sense and determination to see that we in this country put a stop to children begging.

Parents who do take their children out begging may think, however, that so long as a child is not abducted or coerced, one should have the right—or the freedom—to have one's child beg. And it's true that while we might not have the freedom to publish or form associations or demonstrate, we definitely have the freedom to beg—but that's only true of adults. And even in their case, freedom is never absolute: If it's time for a large-scale national celebration or if it's within view of some government vanity project, you are not going to be able to beg as you please. In fact, this is all decided by the beggar's parents after weighing up the benefits: They feel that the one or two thousand yuan the two of them make in a regular job is bound to be less than what their child would make from begging. Personally, I think we can ignore the argument that parents are entitled to have their children beg. To be sure, the state doesn't do enough to protect the disadvantaged, but if parents who have disabilities take their children out to beg, it only gives the government an excuse not to ban children from begging and ultimately leads to the abduction of other parents' children.

It's true that in our country it sometimes doesn't matter very much whether or not something is written into law. Many people feel our laws are incomplete, but that's not really true: We pretty much have all the laws we need—the key thing is what parties are involved: when people in power want to do something, laws are not going to stop them, whereas if you infringe on the privileges of the people in power you'll find that the laws are very stringent. But, however you look at it, having a law on the books is better than having none at all.

Secondly, there are really a lot of people with physical handicaps, and it may be that children with handicaps have really no alternative but to beg. This relates to the question of social protections and welfare. If these things are not provided, how do you expect people to survive? Basic benefits are not nearly enough to keep one alive, and if you have a rural residential permit your entitlements are even less—the state's certainly not going to help you raise your child. The state is bound to think instead: I have already been so good to you in not slapping you with a begging tax and a management tax, so how could I ever dream of giving you money to support your child?

If I can just go off on a tangent for a moment, we all know that our government is very rich. Many people are having a good laugh at the financial crisis in the United States and find it hilarious that some American states have enormous budget deficits and are even on the verge of bankruptcy. But if those states were free to impose a new category of tax—if they could throw a barrier across the highway and levy tolls at will, level a housing tract whenever they feel like it and sell off the land they have cleared, then those state governments wouldn't be in such a mess. Actually, the state governments don't even need to do those things—so long as they collect their normal revenue but dispense only the welfare benefits that Chinese people get, I can guarantee that none of them will go bankrupt. So it is that in countries where governments are prone to going bankrupt, the people themselves can avoid bankruptcy. Unfortunately, some of our people are thrilled to see other governments go bankrupt. They get so excited that they shake awake their wives, who have gotten sick from overwork but dare not go to the hospital for treatment, and tell them, "Our government is really kicking ass . . . ass! . . . ass! . . . ass!" Not much you can do about that echo—when you're living under the arch of a bridge, it comes with the territory.

Finally, we hope that a ban on children begging can finally be written into law and strictly enforced. Many children who have been kidnapped, of course, are simply sold to other people and do not beg in the streets at all, but it still makes sense to start with the problems which are easier to solve before moving on to the more troublesome ones. In an effort to comply with "national policy" and ease the state's burden, so many couples in China have only one child, and now if the government proves incapable of protecting that one child of theirs, then even though you guys never run the slightest risk of bankruptcy you'll still be too embarrassed to face those docile, tongue-tied citizens of yours.

Prices are going to take a dive

February 22, 2011

Recently I keep finding I don't have much money in my wallet—maybe just a few ten-yuan notes are all I find at the end of the day. That easily covers a bowl of noodles, of course. *What happened to all the money I left the house with*, I wonder. Then I realized it's because it costs six hundred yuan to refuel my car, and it costs two or three hundred yuan to treat a few friends to dinner, and it costs fifty yuan to go and come back on the freeway. So long as I don't buy anything extra for myself, one thousand yuan pretty much covers a day's expenses.

I can't help but wonder how those people who just make two or three thousand yuan a month manage to get by in this city. They don't need to buy gas, you may point out, but they've got to get through thirty days a month, after all, and pay for their housing. They have no claim on most of the facilities in this city, so all they can do is look. It's just as well that our government has been compassionate enough to refrain from charging an eye maintenance tax for the privilege of looking at the city.

It was back in 2000, when I'd just published my first book, that I bought a Volkswagen Passat, because in those days that was one of the few models available (along with the Santana and Jetta), and the Passat seemed the most fashionable. Gas was then three yuan a liter and you could fill the tank for a hundred-odd yuan. That was when I developed the habit of leaving home with a thousand yuan, which in those days would have been enough to take me practically all the way to Europe. My parents wanted me to buy an apartment, not so as to improve my living arrangements or invest in real estate but because Shanghai's housing market was in the doldrums, so the government had hatched a scheme whereby you would get a tax refund if you bought property. Housing prices in the outskirts of Shanghai cost between several hundred and a thousand yuan a square meter, and in the city center they were asking three thousand yuan a square meter. "Those prices are outrageous," I said. "To buy a one hundred-square-meter apartment will cost three hundred thousand yuan. At this rate people will have to work for well over ten years to afford an apartment. You shouldn't have to work more than five years to buy a small apartment. These prices are twice what they should be, so now's not the time to buy. The price is going to drop any day now, to below a thousand yuan per square meter."

Later, when I went to Hong Kong, I was shocked by the prices there: How could it cost forty or fifty Hong Kong dollars for a simple lunch combo? I found it amazing that a taxi ride in Hong Kong cost the equivalent of well over a hundred yuan. Housing in Hong Kong, I found, cost tens of thousands of yuan per square meter, and a night in a hotel easily cost over a thousand yuan. It was an enormous relief to get back to Shanghai.

In 2001 I went to Beijing and rented an apartment in Wangjing for a thousand yuan a month. I spent all my royalties on practicing driving and upgrading my car, and I almost couldn't afford to rent an apartment. Later, I managed to save fifty thousand yuan and bought an apartment in Guanzhuang, in a development called Berlin Romance. Although it was actually a good distance from there to downtown Beijing, the freeway terminated in the eastern exten-

198

sion of Chang'an Avenue. To keep things simple, I told my parents that I lived at the east end of Chang'an Avenue. They spread the word, and when I went home neighbors would ask me enviously, "I hear you live right next to Tiananmen—do you get to see the top leaders?"

"I don't see them very often," I said, "but I can smell them. Every time the expressway is closed to ordinary motorists, I know that our leaders are going out, and when we're finally given the all-clear I can smell the exhaust fumes their cars left when they passed ten minutes before."

At that time gas was still over three yuan a liter. "It costs too much," I told my friends. "We shouldn't have to pay more than one yuan. Otherwise people will have to spend a whole month's wages just to keep a car in operation." In those days the Xinyuanli suburb of Beijing was crawling with women who'd gone to the bad: If you wanted to go to the bad with one of them it would cost you only a hundred and fifty yuan, and if you wanted to go to the bad for a whole night it would cost you two hundred.

Later, because I felt lost in Beijing and was in danger of going to the bad myself, I returned to Shanghai, renting a two-bedroom apartment in Songjiang for three thousand yuan a month. Gas cost over four yuan a liter then. "If it goes up to five yuan," I told my friends, "that's a complete joke."

At that time there were no five-star hotels in Songjiang. My apartment was in Kaiyuan Xindu, a new development opposite the university. There houses cost five thousand yuan a square meter. "Why don't you buy an apartment?" a friend asked.

But at that time I couldn't afford one. I would pass the densely packed new developments in Songjiang, where every unit had been sold and only one in a hundred was occupied, and would say to my friend, "There's bound to be a housing collapse, with all this over-building. Five thousand yuan per square meter—they've got to be kidding! Most people would have to work twenty years before they could afford a two-bedroom apartment. Just wait, sooner or later housing prices will slump here in Songjiang, and you'll be able to buy at five hundred yuan a square meter. That's when I'm going to make my move."

"What you say makes a lot of sense," my friend said. "I'd be ruined if I bought a place now. I need to wait it out. Thanks for showing me the light!"

Later, I did buy a house for my parents, spending all my savings on a three-bedroom apartment in Zhongshan in Jinshan District. I'm still fond of that apartment, for though it's not very big, it's a nice design. There was a salon down on the first floor—ten yuan for a hair wash, five yuan for a carwash, and thirty yuan for a hair job. I had taken a break from writing at that point and only just started car racing. After a difficult trial period I joined the best race team in the country, drawing a salary of eighty thousand yuan, but because of a series of unlucky accidents I ended up in fourth place and missed out on a bonus, but still managed to clear a hundred thousand over the course of a year with the help of book royalties. I was content with my life then. I had some regrets about buying property when the market was at its peak, but felt it was worth it to see that my parents got a nice place sooner rather than later. I pretty much forgot about the little apartment in Beijing, thinking that lousy place would soon be down below the one thousand mark, so best simply not to think about it.

That year we experienced a shocking event: Gas prices soared above five yuan a liter. *They'll be taking to the streets in protest*, I thought. But of course I was wrong. We have such great citizens— you're really a lucky devil if China is the country you get to rule.

I needn't go into all the details of how housing prices continued to skyrocket in the years that followed. I never saw that guy who was determined to hold off on a house purchase again. These days my friends often like to recall my confident prediction that house prices would drop below a thousand yuan a square meter. "Your hunch was actually dead right," one of them said to me. "Prices really have fallen below a thousand—but not house prices, stock prices." Poor guy—taking to heart my advice to wait until house prices dropped, he had invested in the stock market, instead.

Today gas prices are close to ten yuan a liter. But they should be higher still, so high that those troublemakers who are so irresponsible and so indifferent to the interests of our leaders as to set fire to themselves at the slightest provocation will not be able to afford to buy even a single liter of gasoline, and housing prices should be a lot higher, too, so high as to be completely out of reach, for that way those girls who are dead set on having a house of their own will marry only rich guys, thereby freeing up China's bachelors to focus all their energies on their jobs, without any further distractions. The tax rate, too, should be higher: Personal income tax should be set at eighty percent, and you shouldn't just have to pay property tax when you buy an apartment, you should pay delivery tax when you have a child and environmental protection tax to make up for the government not protecting the environment; those who make money should pay profit tax and those who lose money should pay experience tax and those who lose a parent should pay inheritance tax; drivers should pay carbon emissions tax and adolescents should pay nocturnal emissions tax and both sexes should pay sexual activity tax. As for why that is better, don't ask me—all I know is that when I was little I saw it written on the wall in big red characters: PAYING TAXES IS GLORIOUS!* And you don't mess with people who have the power to write that kind of slogan.

As for myself, I'm still in the habit of leaving home with a thousand yuan in my pocket. But when I went to Hong Kong a few days ago I was taken aback how cheap things were there. Today I asked for an ice cream cone at KFC and gave the girl two yuan. "That's three yuan," she said. Maybe because KFC and McDonald's haven't raised their prices much, I'm still accustomed to thinking that burgers cost just ten yuan. But there's one happy piece of news. Today,

---

* A sardonic echo of the catchphrase associated with the economic reforms inaugurated by Deng Xiaoping, "Getting rich is glorious."

as housing prices and gas prices and utility prices are all going up,
there is one expenditure that the government has slashed by almost
half. Typically it raises prices by ten or twenty percent, but now I
find it can be very generous when it thinks it necessary. Yes, the
marriage registration fee has been reduced from nine yuan to five.
In other words, if you marry three times in the course of your life,
the government will have saved you a full twelve yuan! Thanks a lot
for that.

Huang Yibo is a fine cadre

May 4, 2011

Recently I was stunned to hear about Huang Yibo, who wears a badge with a full five stripes on it signifying his achievements as a member of the Young Pioneers.* It gives me a real inferiority complex. When I was at school I only made it to two stripes, although I did almost once make it to three. In the class elections in my primary school, a classmate and I were both equally popular candidates, but I ended up with one more vote than she, and the teacher ascribed this to me being too competitive and voting for myself. The result was that she was elected instead of me, and I missed out on my third stripe. I was always under the impression that two bars put me up near the top third, but now I realize I never made it out of the bottom forty percent.

Everyone's now making fun of Huang Yibo and his parents, but I can't go along with this. My experience of holding a student leader-

---

* Huang Yibo, thirteen years old in 2011 and a leading activist in the Wuhan branch of the Young Pioneers of China—a primary-school branch of the Communist Youth League—became the subject of much comment on the Internet in China after a series of promotional photos was posted online.

ship post at school has made me realize how fragile the mentality shaped by the nightly TV news broadcast on state television is. And that experience has never provided any confidence-boosting capital to us after we grow up or fostered any genuine class consciousness — years later when we have a student reunion, it's the person who makes the most money who is everyone's role model and no one commands respect for having once held a post in school. When I was in school, the TV in our classroom was used exclusively for watching the news broadcast, and the papers we subscribed to were *Red Scarf*, *Shanghai High School*, *Global Times*, and *Reference News*. So in those days we were all hoping that war would break out with the United States, and I was convinced that as soon as the People's Liberation Army brought into action the secret weapon they had stashed away in the mountains, U.S. imperialism would suffer a crushing defeat. I continued to have that fantasy about China's advanced technology for years after I graduated, until I became a race car driver and realized that China can't even manufacture a durable ball bearing or hydraulic valve, let alone a decent internal-combustion engine. I realized then that we had no secret weapon at all, and began to worry: If there really is a war, how are we going to manage? In the end I realized that our national defense strategy is not geared toward guarding against foreign armed forces but toward maintaining readiness against the people of our own country.

Even if we concede the possibility that after Huang Yibo grows up he will stay just the way he is now and proceed to serve in officialdom, I have every reason to believe that he will be a good cadre — although, perhaps, a frustrated one. If he started watching network news when he was two and started reading *People's Daily* when he was seven, he has to have an instinctive love of this regime, a love of this political party, a love for the people who inhabit this land. But the cruel history of power struggles in our country tells us that the more you love this party and the more that you try to act in the best interests of this regime, the more quickly you will be purged. Our young friend Huang Yibo doesn't realize that in

China, to be a successful administrator, there are three things you have to remember:

1. You can't love this party.
2. You can't love this country.
3. You can't love this people.

Once you've mastered these three "can't loves," and have paired off with the right interest group, you have a good chance of a flourishing career in the bureaucracy. Classmate Huang Yibo innocently believes everything that the network news and *People's Daily* tell him, but the problem is that the leaders themselves don't believe a word they say—Huang Yibo is the only true believer. So we have every reason to predict that Huang Yibo will find himself elbowed out in the future. Because among a bunch of people who don't believe any of this stuff and just want to use their position to get some benefits, he is going to stick out like a sore thumb.

Secondly, although Huang Yibo's posture may strike us as ridiculous, it's in a child's nature to act that way. When I was young, for example, I used to watch a TV series about the Qianlong Emperor. Thereafter, I would imitate Qianlong and stroll about all day with a fan in my hand, longing to hit somebody with it. After watching all these broadcasts of network news, Huang Yibo naturally is imitating those high-up leaders he's seen so many pictures of. Although his mimicry is not entirely convincing, the way he holds himself does remind one of the mannerisms of a provincial city-level bureaucrat. His body type already shows some similarities, so that whereas his classmates' physical ideal is shaped by their manga heroes, his idea of good looks is probably that beer belly you see leaders sporting— but that, too, is an expression of individuality. And there's nothing wrong with watching network news from an early age. Many people fear that politics may be detrimental to the outlook of primary school children, but I think that the fairy tales you see on network news are actually perfectly appropriate for young minds. And any real effects from prepubescent brainwashing will be scattered to the four winds after the children have experienced adolescence, and will even recoil with a vengeance. Which of us hasn't felt the reverse effects of all that education? What's more, Huang Yibo is kind to the elderly—one has to admire how he went out of his way to visit an old people's home and take an interest in the residents, even without a television camera following him around.

And I don't feel that Huang Yibo has lost out on his childhood. Everyone has their own idol, and ours were hard to emulate, because we couldn't fly around the universe, changing shape and demonstrating miraculous powers like our manga models, so our childhood was a disappointment, whereas Huang Yibo's idols are easy to imitate—all their activities involve is inspecting Unit A and inspecting Facility B, reading this document and reading that, meeting here and meeting there, issuing a directive now and another one later, and wrapping things up with a lot of empty platitudes, so Huang Yibo's childhood is a happy one. It must give him a great sense of satisfaction that he and his idols can merge together so completely. Not only that, but he has got recognition as well—that five-bar badge which makes him the incarnation of an official. Huang Yibo is doing things he loves, so his childhood must be a total delight. We, on the other hand, were miserable, because nobody believed us when we told them we were incarnations of the manga knights, and we kept having to do things we hated.

What a shame that, just as I was writing this essay, the Young Pioneers of the National Youth Work Commission issued a statement to the effect that they have never authorized the award of five stripes, that this innovation is entirely the brainchild of the local Wuhan committee, and that it has no institutional basis. Reading this report, I'm upset on Huang Yibo's behalf. He has done so much, developing an image so close to that of the central leadership, but he has failed to win their recognition and has ended up simply as Wuhan's guinea pig, one that has created tension between province and center. Little did Huang Yibo realize that these five stripes have created extraordinary complications for the Youth Commission. The organization never cares for controversial characters, and it's bound to be seen as ominous when Huang Yibo's school in Wuhan is called Slippery Slope Primary School. The leadership sets a lot of store by auspicious signs and names, and this unfortunate Slippery Slope has really cramped Huang Yibo's style. It's a fair guess that he won't be progressing any further in the Young Pioneers' leadership.

I wish him luck in the Communist Youth League, however.

Three Gorges is a fine dam

May 22, 2011

Recently, the Three Gorges Dam has come under a lot of criticism. Many people have deep concerns about the project, claiming that it is likely to trigger earthquakes, disrupt ecological balance, or provoke drought, and as a way of emphasizing the gravity of the crisis they cite Huang Wanli's prediction that sooner or later the dam will have to be demolished. As a staunch supporter of the Three Gorges dam, I am convinced there is no substance to any of these fears; not only do the dam's advantages outweigh its disadvantages, but its advantages are legion and its disadvantages nonexistent!

As everyone knows, the Three Gorges project* was surrounded by controversy from the start, to the point that it attracted several hundred negative votes and abstentions at the National People's Cheerleading Congress, something that only happens once every hundred years. But these objections failed to prevent the project from going ahead. The dam on the Yangtze, like the aircraft carrier commissioned by our navy, is without question an iconic symbol of

---

* Construction was completed in 2006.

China's national strength. In this essay, I will refute the criticisms one by one.

Critics tell us that the dam will degrade the environment in both the upper and the lower reaches of the Yangtze. But before the dam was built the environment was already degraded, so there is no merit to this criticism.

Critics tell us that the dam will become a huge, sitting target for a military attack and a strike against it would wreak havoc on the power supply and the inhabitants of the lower Yangtze valley. I believe we have already resolved this issue in the most satisfactory manner possible. We have installed numerous enterprises like Foxconn in the cities of the lower Yangtze, and if the dam was blown up and those cities were inundated, the world would be unable to enjoy the fruits of China's cheap labor and—most important—the U.S. imperialists would be unable to manufacture the iPhone. Just that point alone is enough to discourage foreign adversaries from attacking the Three Gorges Dam.

Critics tell us that the dam will trigger earthquakes. First of all, this is just speculation, and it cannot be proven. Second, even if we entertain for a moment the possibility that the Wenchuan earthquake was caused by the Three Gorges Dam—well, didn't you see that at the various events commemorating the third anniversary of the earthquake the emphasis was all on the miraculous reconstruction efforts? For us, the earthquake prompts no reflection— instead, it is an occasion for celebrating triumph. Thinking through this logically, then, we can conclude that the Three Gorges Dam has simply triggered Chinese miracles and in so doing has achieved a wonderful victory—could there be anything in the world better than that?

Critics tell us that the dam will provoke drought. This year, China's largest freshwater lake—Boyang Lake—has only ten percent of the water that it used to have, and many people find this very worrisome and assume that the Jiangxi provincial government must be terribly concerned. They are missing the point entirely. Local government revenue depends largely on the sale of real estate, and a lake with water in it can't be parceled off and sold. What Jiangxi Province should do is seize the opportunity and dam the headwaters of Boyang Lake, getting rid of that remaining ten percent—that way, the provincial government will soon have tens of thousands of square miles more land to sell off! And a slogan like "Original Site of Boyang Lake" will make a great selling point and be a godsend for advertising—"Fertile Spring," "Bountiful Basin"—they'll be raking in the cash! Then all they need to do is invite one of the old gentlemen who pushed the Three Gorges Dam project through and have him draw a circle around where Boyang Lake used to be and make that a Special Economic Zone—that would be another splendid exploit, a huge boost to the hinterland economy.

Some people use the Three Gorges Dam to attack some of our leaders, claiming that their mentality is "Once I'm dead, what does it matter if there's a catastrophic flood?" I want these vicious naysayers to know that the leaders actually see things completely the other way around: It's because the leaders were afraid there'd be a catastrophic flood after they were dead that they were so determined to build the Three Gorges Dam. That way, the worst that can happen is that there's flooding above the dam. So long as there's no flood below the dam, there will always be shrimp to eat. Therefore, this claim of theirs is also untenable.

In short, the Three Gorges Dam is all positives and no negatives—who can go on criticizing it now?

I have a good life
in Shanghai

June 24, 2011

The other day I came back from the airport, and with nothing to
do in the evening I thought I might as well go out and buy a few videos. It had rained, but the skies were clearing and the air was sweet,
so I opened the windows and the moonroof and cruised along in
a leisurely way. There wasn't much traffic as I slipped onto the A8
Freeway. These past few years we've got into the habit of calling
the Shanghai-Hangzhou Expressway the A8, the Shanghai-Qingpu
Expressway the A9, and the ring road the A20, but now they've become the Shanghai-Kunming G60, the Shanghai-Chongqing G50,
and the G1501. I managed to drive these roads for two years without
registering the change.

Before I got very far on the expressway I was forced off, so that
they could do after-midnight maintenance. I dawdled along on sur-
face streets until I got to the elevated expressway above Yan'an Road,
where I suddenly got the idea of going to have a look at "Asia's No. 1

Curve." * As I got close to the Bund I activated the camera feature on my phone, followed the original direction of the road—and ended up in a tunnel. It wasn't until I recalled a news item from a few weeks before that I realized that "Asia's No. 1 Curve" is no more. Somehow that reminded me that my old primary school no longer exists either, and I couldn't help feel disconsolate. But when I thought of how a friend of mine's primary school, middle school, high school, kindergarten, old home, paternal grandparents' home, and maternal grandparents' home all no longer exist, I had to cheer up. Shanghai people aren't in a position to miss their native city, someone has remarked. But perhaps that's true of all Chinese people. They leave their native districts in search of a better life, and if they don't succeed they will wander here and there forever, and if they succeed they'll put down roots somewhere else. The ones who hanker to reconnect with their past come back to find that their old homes have vanished, while the people who don't care simply have no interest in going back at all. People who were born in big cities are maybe better off, because their old homes are not in another part of the country, but you find that even the vestiges associated with your growing up are gone. Often a passenger in my car will say, "Hey, my primary school used to be there!" I look out the window, and it turns out to be luxury apartments.

The only way I can console such people is to tell them: "I heard that someone asked a foreigner living in Shanghai, 'Where are you from?' The guy answered sadly, 'What was once Yugoslavia.'"

At least this city hasn't changed its name, so we can be thankful for that.

When I came out of the tunnel, I was relieved to see at least the Bund still standing. A bit farther on, I found Shanghai now has a Waldorf. As long as you're rich, it seems, you'll be happy here. I

---

* "Asia's No. 1 Curve" was the name given to the curved ramp that used to connect the east-west Yan'an Elevated Road with Zhongshan Road, the boulevard that runs along the Huangpu River, next to the Bund. The ramp was demolished as part of an ambitious plan to ease traffic congestion.

crossed Huaihai Road and found myself in Luwan District—only to realize it no longer exists. Although I was born a country boy, I came to have a deep feeling for Luwan District, because I would have meetings there when I came into the city for business, but now it's become Huangpu District. As I approached Xintiandi, I felt a bit uncomfortable.* After all, it's said that the site of the Chinese Communist Party's First Congress was here, but if the Party isn't worried about it, then what have we to worry about? We're used to this, anyway—things that should be reformed don't get reformed, and things that shouldn't get reformed do. I had the idea of following Huaihai Road and then Huashan Road down to Xujiahui, but found more roadwork in the way, so I decided instead to head for Gubei, where there's a video store that stays open late.

Gubei is one of Shanghai's most posh residential areas, with a big expatriate population—I guess because it's close to the airport, and if things ever get out of hand the foreigners can get to the airport in double quick time. I pulled over to the side of the road, only to be accosted by a drunken youth: "Who said you could park here? Do you think you can park anywhere you like, just because you have a smart car? Get out of here! Scram!"

The shop I was looking for had already closed, so I did scram, and crossing Xianxia Road I saw three young women, also a bit the worse for drink. They were staggering along the street, clutching each other. When I pulled over to another video shop a few hundred yards farther on, they shouted at me, "You rich people think you're so great, with your fancy cars. You're just trash, the whole lot of you!"

I couldn't help but look back at my car. A standard mid-range black sedan in this city full of big-name automobiles—is it really all that fancy? Perhaps because I normally drive with windows closed,

---

* Xintiandi is a small, consumer-oriented district in central Shanghai that appeals to some foreigners and affluent young Chinese; incongruously, the site of the first congress of the Chinese Communist Party is located almost next door.

I just never heard this kind of comment before. I don't know why they were so down in the dumps, but then if I had a difficult life in this city I might need an opportunity to blow off steam, too. Almost immediately a white Lamborghini convertible roared past, with a young woman in her twenties at the wheel. I spun around, fearful to see the girls' reaction, only to find one of them throwing up with one hand on the wall, the other two patting her on the back, so none of them had seen.

In front of the video store was a stretch of grass where a young man was picking up discarded plastic water bottles and stuffing them into two sacks. He turned around as I walked past and I noticed he was wearing a cap and a face mask, the cap pushed down low over his eyes. Clearly he didn't want to do this during the day, and didn't want to be seen. *He and those other young people,* I thought, *perhaps belong to that huge class of disadvantaged who text their families and say, "I have a good life here in Shanghai."* When I entered the video store, a young guy behind the desk greeted me. "Hey there, handsome. Have you seen *The Consolidation of the Party?*" *

"Oh, yes," I told him. "I watch it all the time."

---

* This made-up film title mockingly echoes the title of the 2009 film *The Founding of a Republic.*

The disconnected nation

July 26, 2011

> On July 23, 2011, *two high-speed trains collided near Wenzhou, in Zhejiang Province, killing dozens of passengers and injuring many more. The authorities brought rescue operations to a rapid halt, burying the derailed carriages, and attempted to restrict media coverage.*

You never stop asking: Why do they always have to misrepresent the facts? But they feel they could hardly be more candid and fair.

You never stop asking: Why do they always have to shield the offender? But they feel they've let their buddy down.

You never stop asking: Why do they always have to cover up the truth? But they feel they could hardly be more transparent and open.

You never stop asking: Why do they always have to lead such corrupt lives? But they feel they could hardly live in a more simple, spartan way.

You never stop asking: Why do they always have to be so overbearing and arrogant? But they feel they could hardly have a more humble attitude.

You feel aggrieved, but they feel aggrieved, too. Under the Qing government a hundred years ago, they recall, the common people never got to see television at all, whereas now everyone has a television—what a big step forward this is!

We built this, they think, and we built that. You don't need to concern yourselves with what happened in the process or whose palms were greased—you got to enjoy it, didn't you? It used to take a day and a night to get from Shanghai to Beijing, and now—so long as the train's not struck by lightning—you can make the trip in five hours. Why aren't you grateful? Why do you raise so many questions?

Why can't our country progress? It's because so many of our officials consistently judge themselves by the standard of the Mao or the Stalin era, and so they always feel aggrieved: In their eyes, they're so enlightened, so just, so generous, so unassuming—and that's a tremendous achievement! It's not that technological advances are pushing society forward, they think—no, it's all because of their conscious decision to open things up. So the more you criticize them, the more they long for absolute power, the more you mock, the more they want to be Mao.

"You're just never satisfied," an official told me. "A literary type like you—if you'd been around forty years ago, you'd have been shot. That's a sign of progress, no?"

"You're the ones who're never satisfied," I said. "If you'd expressed that kind of view ninety years ago, you'd have been laughed off the streets." Are we really seeing progress here?

Yes, an accident did happen, they concede, but the top leadership expressed its concern. We also sent someone to answer you reporters' questions. The original compensation was set at one hundred seventy thousand yuan, and now it has been raised to five hundred thousand, and we even sacked one of our best buddies. We really went the extra mile, so why do you keep harping on about little details, why don't you lighten up a bit? How come you've lost your sense of the big picture? Why do you want us to apologize? We have committed no crime—an accident like this is just the price you pay when you develop. Disposing of the bodies so rapidly—well, that's just standard operating procedure; early signing-off on the death certificate leads to a bigger bonus, late signing-off leads to less compensation—that's the method our sister department found so effective when conducting forcible demolition and resettlement. To bury the train carriages was a poor decision, yes, but it came from higher up, because they wanted any potential source of trouble hidden on the spot. The mistake we made was to do the job in broad daylight and make too big a hole, and we didn't communicate adequately with the propaganda department or fully control the photographers in the area, so our preparatory work was a bit rushed. The biggest lesson we learned from this accident is that in the future when burying things we need to take their size into account and also the secrecy of the work. These things we underestimated.

But generally speaking, they feel, the rescue operation was successful and timely. Deployment of resources was reasonable, the overall plan was normal, and the handling of the aftermath was satisfactory. The only unfortunate aspect was that public opinion got a bit out of control. But that's not our responsibility, they feel—public opinion is not under our control.

If you look at the big things, they think, we held the Olympics, we eliminated taxes on farmers, but you don't give us credit for all that stuff, you're always picking on little details here and there—just what are you getting at? We could easily have been more repressive politically than North Korea, more impoverished economically than Sudan, more ruthless organizationally than the Khmer Rouge, because we have a bigger army than all of them put together, but we didn't do things that way. Not only are you not grateful, but you want us to apologize. We feel so misused.

In this nation of ours, everybody feels aggrieved—the rich and the poor, the powerful and the powerless alike. In a nation where

219

everyone feels aggrieved, the various strata of society all become disconnected from each other and every component part of this huge country just keeps coasting on, carried along by its inbuilt momentum. Without reform, we'll find that disconnection is not our biggest problem — it's going off the rails that we need to worry about.

What do you do if it's too downbeat?

──────────

November 2, 2011

This is the first time I've written anything since "The Disconnected Nation" was erased from my blog. I'm not the most diligent author in the first place, and when I post something one day and it is gone the next, it really puts a damper on my mood. Sometimes you can't help feeling you have all the cards stacked against you: There's such a multiplicity of government departments that even if the propaganda department and the news publication department think there's no problem, any other department equipped with a level of sedan higher than a Volkswagen Passat can get rid of an essay with a single telephone call. The most restrained of them has to be the provincial public security department that waited a whole year to delete an essay I had posted back in 2008. No wonder people are always saying that public security takes its time about responding to complaints! When there are so many agencies with the power to shut you up, it's a real brainteaser to work out how to write anything at all.

After engaging in this line of work for some thirteen years now, I realize that creative artists, in terms of the status they hold, are a useless, pathetic bunch. Because of all the limitations placed on the fruits of their labor, there's no way they can come out with their best work.

In the Chinese publishing industry, there's actually no official censorship. This may come as a big surprise to you, because it flies in the face of common sense. But every year hundreds of thousands of books are published in China, and there's no way they can all be inspected. And I'm sure that most of the comrades who make it their business to keep an eye on writers don't actually care much for reading, so in practice censorship is something that the publishing houses themselves attend to, in the form of retrospective censorship. This is even more of a jolt to the system than preemptive censorship—a blunter instrument, with more negative effects. Friends who have resorted to morning-after contraceptives will surely know what I mean.

But you need a book number to be able to publish, and only publishing houses can issue book numbers, and only with official approval can you have a publishing house, so from the very start it's impossible to have free publishing in China. Since many state-owned publishing houses are in poor shape, independent companies have begun to get involved in publishing, either in partnership with state-owned companies or by buying book numbers from other publishers. But this does not alter the status quo, because the publisher remains the final inspection agency. In the past, if a book could not be published, the justification given was that it was counterrevolutionary. Later, the word *counterrevolutionary* dropped out of use, because if to be counterrevolutionary is something bad, that would seem to encourage revolution. But the official view, of course, is that the work of revolution is already finished, so although we certainly don't want counterrevolution, we can't have revolution, either—the best outcome is that things just stay as they are. So, the reason we are given these days for a book being banned is that it's too downbeat. My first book, *Triple Door*, for instance, took forever to be published because it was too downbeat. *Downbeat* is a fatal flaw, because you can always revise something that's a bit sloppy or straighten out the kinks in a ropey argument. But that which is *downbeat* gives you a real headache, because you've got no idea how to make the downbeat go up. If you ask the publisher what he means by *downbeat*, he doesn't know, either, and it's only now I realize that what *downbeat* means is "beat down."

I have always suffered at the hands of censorship. But when I up my beat a little, with a bit of luck I can publish my work, and because it sells well I can sometimes manage to get the publisher's permission to be a bit more downbeat on some minor points here and there. Every time I write, I first have to engage in some self-censorship. People who've never engaged in this line of work tend to feel that we're too wimpy, that we don't have enough spunk. When I ran into a lot of difficulties trying to publish the magazine *Party*, for example, some friends lost patience with me. "You're such a dork," they said. "If it was me, I wouldn't ask for a number, I'd just take the files down to the printers and print a couple of hundred thousand copies right there, and put them on the market." I admire their gumption, but what they don't realize is that the printer won't start the press rolling until they get authorization from the publisher. Without that clearance, not only will you be unable to print a single copy, but you'll also be having a tête-à-tête with the police before you know it. Even if your dad runs a printing press and you get him to run off two hundred thousand copies, you still don't have a book number, so no bookstore or newspaper kiosk will accept your stuff—not even the ones that are comfortable selling pirated goods. "Well, then," you say, "I'll put it up on the web, I'll sell it on Taobao." Well, I'll tell you, if you want to sell books on Taobao, first of all you need to have the finances, and secondly you can't just display the cover and start selling the book right away—you need to tap in the book number, and it's only when the system matches your book number and the book title that you can post things for sale.

So now, as in the past, writers have to grit their teeth and censor themselves. Can we perhaps hope to find a publishing house that might be willing to lower its tone? No, that's not in the cards at all. A publishing house is a state-owned enterprise, and as soon as it shows signs of lowering its tone all the government needs to do is assign a new executive to run it, while the comrades who lowered the tone end their days in the All-China's Women's Federation or the China Disabled Persons' Federation. The most awful element in retrospective censorship is the punishment phase: I'm not going to interfere, but if you dare to publish something shady, I'll see that you suffer. If I'm in a good mood I'll see you lose your job and get kicked out of the company altogether, and if I'm in a bad mood then I'll throw you in jail—so do as you think best.

In my own case, although every essay has undergone self-censorship and emasculation, inevitably it sometimes happens that even in this bowdlerized form it still fails to pass muster and inflicts too much stress on the publishing house. My latest novel, for example, got the thumbs down, because its protagonist is surnamed Hu. Even if I've only written five thousand words so far, the publisher is convinced it must be a political allegory. When I realized I should have avoided this taboo, it was already too late. But in observing taboos you can't afford to forget previous leaders. In another one of my novels, because I wrote a phrase in which both the characters Jiang and Hu appeared, it was shot down all the more quickly, for this was doubly offensive.

What a fool I am—I know I can't afford to upset these people, so why couldn't I keep out of their way? I don't know how a country where a writer starts shaking as soon as he picks up his pen can become a cultural powerhouse, or how a country where one can't find the Tang poet Li Bai on Google because his name infringes on the name of a Politburo Standing Committee member can become a cultural powerhouse, either.* I have no clue how to go about reforming our cultural system, and have one simple wish—that Han Zheng, the mayor of Shanghai, won't climb any higher in the bureaucracy. If he does, I won't be able to Google myself.

_224_

---

* According to a leaked diplomatic cable, Politburo Standing Committee member Li Changchun was shocked to discover results critical of himself when he conducted a Google search and typed in his own name.

We already had our say on that

November 16, 2011

I have been keeping a blog now for six or seven years, and even though I have been far from assiduous in updating it I find that I've now written several hundred posts in all. But as time has gone on a good half of Chinese bloggers have transferred their attention to social networking sites, while the other half have become converts to microblogs of one kind or another. For the past year or so, the links on the left of my screen have been left unattended—it's not just a case of tea going cold when someone leaves, for the tea has completely dried up, leaving only the cup itself. Most of those former bloggers have probably already forgotten their own username and password. But I like it better this way. It's as though a bunch of people suddenly came crowding in, doing the same thing as you, then left again just as suddenly. You don't feel lonely when they're gone—it just seems tidier.

"Why don't *you* have a microblog?" people ask. Actually, I did do one for a few days, but soon came to feel it didn't suit me, so I closed down the account. It's not that I found the 140-character limit too restrictive, for who would insist on always writing an essay ten times that length? A regular essay requires quite a bit of thought, whereas with a microblog post just three or four neatly put sentences are all that's needed. On days when you can't think of anything to say, you can make do just by forwarding other people's posts. What I found was that after about a week of microblogging a change seemed to have come over me. First of all, I couldn't help constantly checking how many times my posts had been forwarded and how many new fans I had and how many people had made a positive or negative comment on something I had written. The person who bad-mouthed me has an officially verified account—what's their background, I wonder. This one who praised me has a picture and is really quite a looker—I wonder where she lives? Hey, she's really cute—how about if I put a "Follows" tag on her—that way she's bound to respond by sending me a personal message, and after a bit of back and forth we can set up a date or something. Oh, what a tragic story here! That's just terrible. I don't have too much to say about it, but I'll forward a note deploring what happened, and that should satisfy my readers' expectations—I am supposed to be the scourge of all evil, after all. Hey, that pretty girl has sent me a message, so now I'm going to have a look at her web page and get a sense of her lifestyle, but I mustn't get carried away. Oh, and now a friend wants me to pass on the news that he has a new book out. Hey, that tragedy now turns out to be just fake news—shit, it sounded so convincing. Wow, so many people are singing my praises, I'll send off a note thanking them. Right, this guy thinks I'm cool, too, and he's got a good brain and good looks, so I maybe shouldn't leave a comment after his, but rather forward his comment and then express appreciation, so that way even more people will see how he praised me—that's doesn't count as shameless, after all, since it leaves everyone happy. Oh, it looks like that tragedy really did happen—Sina has confirmed it, so I better hurry up and make a quick comment on it—if it turns out to be fake news then I can blame it on Sina. Oh, here's another tragic story, I'll forward it—hey, hang on, if I forward it, maybe that means the guy who sent it to me gets the credit, so perhaps I should rephrase things and say at the start: "I just read this story about something that happened in XX City. . . ." Wouldn't that be better for my figures? And it would also show I don't spend the whole day updating my microblog. Damn it, how can I be thinking that way? Forget it, it's time for bed.

Okay, time to get up. Let's have a look at the comments and update the news. Oh, and don't forget the personal messages. So many newly added followers—no way I can look at them all. Hey, this starlet is a follower, and I have a crush on her. Why don't I flirt with her a bit in a personal message? She wrote a whole post about me in her microblog, so why don't I shoot off a reply to further tickle her interest? Hmm, who is this guy—I think I've seen him somewhere. Let's read this stuff about him. Wow, his company is huge. Oh no, this little girl got terribly burned in that fire, how awful! Better forward that, and donate some money. Maybe I should be writing some insight into life, but I don't seem to have got any new insight into life recently! But shit, I've been at this game for so many years now, I shouldn't have any trouble coming up with some surefire chicken soup for the soul, even if I can't stand those pretentious soul-counselors. Now I've got to go out and do one or two things, but in my spare moments I'll still be able to check my microblog. My friend texts me to tell me he used to know that chick I have my eye on—that's good, I'll make some roundabout inquiries to try to find out how she's placed. Oh, she's married! Damn it, on her microblog she comes across as a lonely single. Okay, so I'll just have a look at my friend's microblog. What, he's forwarded a post about saving dogs transported on the freeway, pleading with everyone to rescue those golden retrievers. Damn it, it wasn't long ago that he ate the family dog for extra energy in the winter!

That's right, writing these things on a microblog makes me feel good, for I am vain and sometimes even a bit hypocritical. As I achieve more in life, I can pretend to be less and less vain, since I have more reason to think highly of myself. But I remain vain internally. To opt out of attending awards ceremonies or upper-crust events is actually just another form of vanity, rather than genuine detachment. After keeping a blog for years now, I'm not easily distracted by people's comments or expectations. But if I keep a microblog for a few days I find myself immersed in a heroic fantasy world. Of course, maybe it's just me who acts that way. Maybe everyone else can write without a second thought, dash things off effortlessly and maintain their composure while displaying their art, without all the second-guessing that I do. But I felt an unhealthy state of mind was affecting me, so I decided to close down my microblog. If you're not a writer, on the other hand, a microblog might be a good way to spice up your life and unveil a better version of yourself.

Microblogs have altered the form and speed with which information is transmitted and have complicated efforts to block it. In reality, of course, it is the Internet that has changed everything, and it's a variety of products that have made communication that much more convenient. I have an alternative online pseudonym that I use regularly to sign in and see what's going on. Actually there's no real difference from before—it's just less trouble to access. I used to get my news from the papers, and I might have to look at twenty newspapers; later I would sign into chat rooms—four or five of them; and now we have microblogs, and so long as I follow enough people's microblogs and they are all to my liking, then all I need is a single account. Although more scandals are publicized than before, the issues go away all the more quickly. When you read the papers, a month or two after an event you still see follow-up, in-depth reports. When I was in middle school, I was under the impression that if a scandal was uncovered it would be a topic of discussion for months. Later, twelve years ago, when I began to join online discussions, I realized just how many things I had been in the dark about before. Now, when you access microblogs you hear about even more things, but unless an event is really tragic, something that is news in the morning will have disappeared from view in the afternoon, and you need to do an online search to find any trace of it. But what I have learned is that, through all this time, I have remained pretty much the same person I was before, and I don't seem to have affected the people around me, who just carry on with their own concerns and interests. I don't think it's the case that my essays have influenced readers' tastes; rather, they have simply been consumed by readers who share the same tastes.

The result, I find, is not that people change, but that like-minded people come together in one place. In my own microblog universe, you're bound to feel that this government is the pits and that its days are numbered. If you read someone else's microblog, you find that life is comfortable and everything is great. And so, the world you see is simply the one that you follow online. And that world is updated so constantly you don't even have time to download it.

There were a couple of days last week when all my time was taken up with motor racing and I didn't go online at all. Only afterward, on the way home, did I check the latest microblog messages. A friend of mine posted something about a tragic incident that happened over a week ago. He had given the matter a lot of thought, done some research, and after seven or eight days came to a certain conclusion about what actually happened. His analysis made a lot of sense and I expressed full agreement. Usually a lot of people forward his messages, but only a few dozen people forwarded this one, and a post on the first page of comments read, "How come there are still people commenting on this? We already had our say on that."

Speaking of revolution

December 23, 2011

Recently I've been looking over questions that readers have sent in, and the topics of revolution and reform have come up repeatedly. The media love to ask me about these things too, but all that happens is that I talk and they listen—there's no way that what I say will appear in a newspaper. Whatever view you take on these issues, you're likely to get in trouble. But here I'm going to devote the whole post to my ideas about revolution, merging together my answers both to readers and the media.

Q. Mass protests have recently been springing up in China. Do
   you think China needs a revolution?
A. In a country whose social makeup is increasingly complex—
   and particularly when that country is in Asia—the final
   winners in a revolution are bound to be ruthless and cruel.
   To be quite frank, revolution is a word which sounds refreshing and exciting and seems to promise instant results,
   but for China it's not necessarily a good choice. For a start,
   a revolution needs to make demands, and demands nor-

mally begin with an attack on corruption. But that kind of demand can't sustain itself very long. Freedom or justice doesn't have a market either, because apart from some writers, artists, and journalists, if you ask the average man or woman in the street if they are free, they generally feel that they are; and if you ask them whether they need justice, the prevailing view is that so long as they personally don't suffer injustice, that's sufficient. It's not everyone who regularly experiences unfair treatment, so they won't identify with efforts to seek justice and freedom for others. In China it's very hard to formulate a demand that has collective appeal. So it's not a question of whether a revolution is needed or not, it's a question of whether it can possibly happen. My view is: It's neither possible nor necessary. But if you ask me whether China needs more substantial reform, my answer is: absolutely.

Q. Why don't you lead an uprising yourself?
A. You've got to be kidding. Even if I identified with revolution and led an uprising in Shanghai and it won widespread support, all the government has to do is shut down the Internet and block cell phone signals, and I bet that without the government even mobilizing its stability-maintenance machine those angry protestors will be so devastated by their inability to chat with their friends through instant messaging or play games on the Internet or watch recordings of soap operas that they'll crush me in no time at all. Don't harbor the fantasy that you can support me by constantly updating the posts on your microblog, because you won't even be able to open the thing, and after three days of that you're going to start hating me.

Q. Do you mean to say that China doesn't need democracy and freedom?

A. There's a lot of confusion about this. Intellectuals tend to think of democracy and freedom as a single package. Actually, for the Chinese, democracy may well lead to a lack of freedom. In the eyes of most Chinese, freedom has nothing to do with publishing, media, and culture, or with personal expression, elections, and politics, but with public standards of behavior. Thus, people with no access to power feel free to make an uproar, jaywalk, and spit, while people with connections feel free to ignore regulations, take advantage of loopholes, and engage in all kinds of malfeasance. Good democracy brings with it social progress and greater respect for the law, and this is bound to make the majority of people — who are not concerned about cultural freedom — feel that they're not as free as before, just as when many Chinese visit developed countries they feel acutely uncomfortable. So democracy and freedom don't necessarily go hand in hand. I feel that Chinese people have their own unique definition of freedom; freedom in the broader sense doesn't get much traction in China.

233

Q. China's problems are just too deeply rooted, so reform is not going to get us anywhere. Only with a revolution can we really turn things around, right?

A. Let's suppose that revolution is allowed to develop and there's no clampdown. No, that's impossible. Let's imagine for a moment that a revolution takes place and makes a certain amount of progress: There's no way that students, ordinary people, the social elite, intellectuals, peasants, and workers can all reach a common understanding. And we always overlook a section of the population — that's to say the poor, who number some two hundred fifty million. Under normal circumstances you wouldn't notice their existence, because they never use the Internet. If a revolution has reached an intermediate stage, it has to have generated a new leader, for a revolution without a leader can't hope to succeed—the White Lotus uprising is a good example. But a revolution with a leader is not necessarily going to be something much to celebrate—the Taiping Rebellion is a good example of that.* A Chinese-style leader is going to be nothing like the kind and humane person that you imagine when you sit there in front of your computer. A Chinese-style leader most likely will be arbitrary and imperious, selfish and crazy, vicious but also an effective demagogue. Hmm, yes, that does sound a bit familiar, doesn't it? But Chinese people will go along with it, and only if you're like that can you climb to the top of the heap, for this society is accustomed to scoundrels ruling the roost and good guys getting the chop. The kind of leaders that young intellectuals would favor would be kicked out within a week, I reckon, and the more educated you are the less likely it is that you would pledge allegiance to a leader. So these people will be the first to abandon the revolution.

With the departure of the social elite, there is bound to be a change in the composition of the revolutionary masses. No matter how appealing the revolution's original slogan, in the end it is bound to boil down to a single word—money. The nice way to put it would be that we're taking back what really belongs to us; the more unpleasant way to put it would be that, in the eyes of an egalitarian, looting is legitimate. I know what you're thinking: Because I've made some money, I'm scared shitless that I'll lose it all. But that's not it. In the surging tide of revolution, if you have an iPhone, if you drive a motorcycle, or even if you just surf the Internet or regularly buy a newspaper and eat at Kentucky Fried Chicken, then

---

* The White Lotus Rebellion in the late eighteenth century and the Taiping Rebellion in the mid-nineteenth century both led to immense destruction and loss of life, and took many years to suppress.

you count as someone with money. So long as you are capable of reading this essay online, that makes you a target for revolution, dripping with original sin. Someone with a fortune of a hundred million yuan is actually safer than someone with property worth ten thousand, because when the richer man opens his door in the morning, his copy of the *New York Times* is sitting right there—he already has a home abroad. In the end, the ones who suffer will be the middle class, the quasi-middle class, and even the quasi-affluent. In the political campaigns of the past, people turned on others and drove them to their deaths, and these days, people have become inured to wrecking other people's lives for the sake of monetary advantage. So just imagine what's going to happen. Plus, we Chinese believe in settling scores, so we are bound to see some violent convulsions.

Any revolution needs time, and with China as big as it is, even setting aside the prospect of nationwide chaos, warlord rivalries, and a power vacuum, if things drag on for five—or ten—years, ordinary working people are bound to look forward to some dictator with an iron fist who can restore order and sort things out. If that entails giving up on liberalization and reverting to *People's Daily* orthodoxy, it won't matter to them. Besides, all our hypotheses are predicated on the army being subordinate to the government rather than the Communist Party, so these are all fantasies, and when even fantasies are not optimistic, the real thing is bound to be ten times worse.

Q. Well, what about Egypt and Libya . . . ?
A. They were both governed for decades by a dictator, and their cities are few. In countries like that, with a single incident as a trigger and a single square as the focus for protests, revolution can succeed. In China, there is no one specific individual who can be the target of revolution—there are many

235

cities and a huge population, and all kinds of shocking disasters have already happened. The G-spot is already numb, never mind the flashpoint. Even if social contradictions were ten times more intense than they are now and even if we had ten Vaclav Havels giving speeches simultaneously in ten different cities, and if we imagine too that the authorities don't interfere, ultimately these speeches will end up becoming advertisements for sore throat lozenges delivered in the Haidian Playhouse.

Of course, all that is beside the point. The most important thing is that most Chinese people wouldn't blink at seeing other people slaughtered, for they cry out only when they personally suffer. It would be impossible for them all to maintain solidarity.

Q. Your position seems just like that of the government's paid minions—has your palm been greased, too? Why can't we elect our president through one-person, one-vote?

A. In a society like this where things are either one way or another, black or white, right or wrong, boss or flunky, the very word *revolution* itself sounds intimidating, and when put into practice it's going to wreak even more havoc. Many people think introducing one-person, one-vote is China's most pressing need, but this is not so. If we do that, the final result is bound to be that the Chinese Communist Party's candidate will win, for who has more money than the CCP? With fifty billion yuan, they can easily buy five hundred million votes. If fifty billion's not enough, they can raise the figure to five hundred billion—the nation's annual tax revenues come to ten trillion, after all. How are you going to compete with that? You feel that the friends in your circle are fair and independent, but adding up all their votes can't amount to more than several hundred thousand ballots, and those enlightened would-be legislators that you admire would be lucky to muster as many as one hundred thousand votes. The only person who can hold his own with the CCP is Ma Huateng,* because he can pop open a window when your instant messaging service starts up and say: "Vote for me and I'll give you five thousand in Q coins." He can certainly count on two hundred million votes by doing that. But the problem is, Ma Huateng will have joined the Communist Party by that point.

Democratization is inevitable, but it's a complex and difficult process, and it is not going to be easily achieved by reciting these mantras that slip off the tongue so smoothly—revolution, general elections, a multi-party system, over-throwing you-know-what. If you have never cared about the independence of the judiciary or about publishing freedoms, being concerned about elections doesn't really amount to much—it simply shows you're drawn to the slogan's sex appeal, a bit like those people who, when they mention car racing, think it's all about Formula 1, or when talking about soccer know only of the World Cup.

237

Q. I feel that in China revolution and democracy are just a mat-ter of timing—what do you think will be the best time?

A. Revolution and democracy are two completely different things. There's no guarantee that revolution will bring democracy—didn't we already establish that a long time ago? History gave China a chance to take the democratic path, and our situation now reflects the choice made by our parents' generation. Of all the countries in the world today, China is the least likely to see a revolution, but the one that most urgently needs reform. If you insist that I tell you the best time for revolution, all I can say is: When everyone

* Ma Huateng is founder of Tencent, Inc., the third largest Internet company in the world after Google and Amazon. Tencent's online currency, Q coins, can be used to buy virtual goods.

knows to dim their headlights when they pass another car on the road, then we'll be ready for a revolution.

But a country like that doesn't actually need a revolution at all. When the people's personal caliber and educational level reach that point, everything will just happen automatically. Perhaps you will see this great change in your lifetime, or perhaps to your dying days you'll just go on being a thread in this huge knot we've tied ourselves into. But in any case, be sure to remember to turn off your high beams — maybe this way our children will sooner achieve what our parents' generation was striving so hard to attain.

Talking about democracy

December 24, 2011

Q. Revolution doesn't necessarily entail violence, does it? Just
think of the Velvet Revolution.

A. I don't think a Velvet Revolution can take place in China.
Let's put aside the issue of the international situation at the
time and the fact that the entire population of Czechoslova-
kia then was just half of what Beijing's is now—to put your
faith in a Velvet Revolution is to choose to trust in the quality
of the people, the acquiescence of those in power, and a
leadership made up of intellectuals. Only with the conflu-
ence of these three elements could the Velvet Revolution
come into being, and I think none of these conditions exist
in China. You can't keep harping on about a perfect revolution as a way of rejecting the prospect of a possibly imperfect
reform. But no matter whether revolution in China is violent
or nonviolent, writers are going to play a lot less important
role than they imagine—and they certainly won't be its leaders. Given the quality of the population at large, it's all the
more unlikely that writers will have any major role to play

at all. You can't just ignore Chinese realities and pontificate about how things should be in terms of perfect democracy, perfect freedom, and perfect human rights. Reform and democracy are actually a process of bargaining—you can't expect the people in power suddenly to see the light and give you everything you want, just because they have read a few books. You can't be constantly anticipating a Velvet Revolution and rehearsing your role as the Chinese Havel, imagining that overnight every person in China will get to vote, and not one of those votes will have been bought. Even today, the Czech Republic does not have universal suffrage. So my view is simple: We don't want a violent revolution, and a Velvet Revolution is not going to happen in China anytime soon. Perfect democracy will never appear in China, so all we can do is to pursue it one step at a time. It's pointless to fantasize about democracy and freedom in the isolation of your study—you'll just drive yourself crazy that way. Gradual reform is the best way out at present.

240

Q. Your conclusion is that the Chinese people's quality is too low, so they're not suited to democracy. You've accepted a kickback from the government's stability-maintenance budget, haven't you?

A. I don't know how you can attribute that conclusion to me. I think I've put it very plainly. Democracy is not something that's suitable or unsuitable—sooner or later, it's bound to come. The low caliber of the people doesn't rule out democracy, but it does decide the quality of democracy when it does arrive. Nobody wants to see a Rwanda-style democracy, although that is not a true democracy in the broad sense. Democracy may come slowly or suddenly, and perhaps it won't be all that thorough or comprehensive, or so American or so European, but it will definitely come in your lifetime, and when we look back it may not seem so dramatic.

Q. Are you saying that everything depends on gifts given by those in power, rather than things taken by the efforts of the people?

A. Of course it's vital to put pressure on those in power, but, sadly, their willingness to compromise is even more important, and that requires a degree of vision on their part, and also sheer luck. Currently, the various levels of society are disconnected. Take the people in power, for example: No matter how much of an uproar the Wenzhou train accident provoked, they are still playing it cool, feeling that this is just a minor flap, that things will calm down of their own accord without any need to take more drastic measures. The families of the people in power may well have absolutely no interest in this incident, caring only about who is going up and who is coming down, who's a bit too young or old, how to rank so-and-so. Even with all the uproar over the train collision, they are going to feel that it will all pass in due course and things will revert to normal. Of course, what's even more likely is that they never felt the pressure of public opinion, a bit like if you have a billion in your bank account, you're not going to panic if you lose a thousand. If you add up all the money in the pockets of the people in cultural circles, it only comes to five hundred yuan, and when they imagine the rulers have just six times that, they are simply creating a false picture of how anxious the rulers must be. Actually, the issues you raise are not even on their radar. But many people in cultural circles think that all our problems are a product of our system, as though everything will be solved as soon as we change it. Although they mean well and have their hearts in the right place, they tend to expect peasants and workers to share their values—or even take it for granted that the whole society should think the same way they do—when the reality on the ground is much more discouraging.

Rally-race venues tend to be in fairly remote areas, so in

241

recent years I've visited over a hundred county towns. None of them, I find, are particularly deprived or cut off from the world. When I talk to their residents, I find that they are not thirsting for democracy and freedom as hungrily as people in cultural circles imagine. Their resentment of authoritarian government and corruption does not lead them to ask, "How can we limit and monitor these things?" but rather "Why can't I, or why can't my family, have what bureaucrats have?" Only when they bear the brunt of some inequity, only when they personally feel the need to protest, will they reach for a dictionary to find those progressive concepts in an effort to protect themselves. So long as the government gives them adequate compensation they'll be satisfied. If a social conflict can be resolved simply by some money changing hands, it's not really much of a problem. But intellectuals tend to regard people's ad-hoc adoption of these fashionable words as the expression of a universal demand and assume that everyone is on the same page. I don't believe there are good prospects for a revolution in a country where there's such a stark divide separating one group of people from another. "If those people are so docile," you may say, "that's just because the government trained them to think that way. So we need change at the top." But this is the reality we're facing, and it's not going to change radically anytime soon. At the same time, I'm not pessimistic, because when I talk with these people's children, the Internet and other kinds of media have broadened their outlook considerably.

The Chinese Communist Party now has eighty million members, and if you throw in all their relatives, that's another three hundred million, so it can't be thought of simply as a political party or a ruling elite. A lot of the time, the Party's shortcomings are the people's shortcomings. A powerful one-party system, it seems to me, amounts in the end to a no-party system, because once a party reaches a certain scale, it takes on the character of the people, just as the people exemplify the system, so the issue is not what we do with the Communist Party—the Communist Party is only a label, just as the system is only a label. To change the people is to change everything. So we need to focus on improvements. The legal system, education, and culture have to be the foundation.

Q. If revolution does come, what role should influential intellectual figures play?

A. They should sit on the fence, but turn their faces against the wind. Intellectuals need to have a sense of justice, but shouldn't be wedded to a single position; the more influential they are the less they should take sides. If they see one faction getting the upper hand they should express support for some other force in society; they should keep their distance from any particular agenda, any particular faith. They need to think of all revolutionaries as potential confidence men and disbelieve all their promises, doing everything possible to ensure that no one party can eliminate others and become dominant. Thus, if China has a revolution in the future, I will stand by whoever is the weaker, and if they become strong, I'll side with their rivals. I'm ready to sacrifice my own view in order to see that different sides coexist. Only that way can we achieve everything we're seeking to accomplish.

Finally, just to be able to discuss these things as the year draws to a close makes for the best possible New Year. This time round, unlike in previous debates, there is no single adversary. I'm grateful to all the friends who have raised issues with me—they are all excellent points. If my answers don't always address the questions, I hope you'll understand.

243

Pressing for freedom

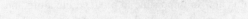

December 26, 2011

A couple of essays ago I said that different people want different freedoms and in my last essay I said that democracy and the rule of law involve a process of bargaining. No matter how big the markdowns in the Christmas sales, you're not going to get something for nothing. So now I need to start doing some bargaining.

For a start, as someone involved in culture, in the coming New Year I demand a freer hand in literary creation. I'm not putting it in terms of freedom of this or freedom of that, because those two expressions will only provoke wariness and alarm in certain quarters, even if these freedoms have always been written into our constitution. In reality, they have never been well implemented. At the same time, on behalf of my colleagues in the media, I need to demand more freedom for the press, since the news is always subject to such rigid controls, and freedom also for my filmmaking friends, who have a terrible time. Working in the cultural arena is like stepping into a minefield—you have to walk slowly, and never in a straight line.

It is in the direction of freedom, after all, that our age is surely moving, and we are not asking for things the government hasn't already promised. I know that you've done your research on the Soviet Union; I know you think a big reason for Communism's collapse there was that Gorbachev relaxed press restrictions and transferred supreme power from the Communist Party to the Congress of People's Deputies, as mandated by the constitution. So this makes you extremely circumspect about freedom of speech and constitutional government. But we live in an era where information moves so freely that trying to block it is futile, and your restrictions on culture simply mean that it is next to impossible to produce literature and cinema that will have any influence in the world. Chinese authors and directors alike are reduced to a state of perpetual embarrassment. China's media, likewise, has no global impact, for there are lots of things that money simply cannot buy. A culture boom is actually the cheapest thing around—the less you try to control culture, the more it is going to flourish. If you continue to insist that Chinese culture is not subject to restraints, that's just too disingenuous. So in the year to come I call upon the authorities to loosen the bonds that are stifling culture, publishing, media, and film.

246

If I see concessions on your side and more freedom in the cultural arena, then on my part I'll try not to settle scores, to look to the future, to steer clear of the most sensitive issues in policy implementation, to withhold comment on high leaders' families and their special interests, and just focus on discussions of current society. Ideally, then, cultural circles and the government can both give a little ground and so enable everyone to have a bit more space.

But if there's no improvement after two or three years, then I will personally make an appearance at every congress of the Writers' Association or the Federation of Literary and Art Circles, to audit the proceedings and register my protest. I know this is a bit like an ant trying to shake a tree, but given the little power I have, that's as much as I can hope to do. Of course, it will just be me—I won't bring anyone else or mobilize my readers to follow my example. I'm not going to use other people's futures to doll up my own résumé.

At the same time, I have faith in the character of the people of our generation, so I believe these freedoms are bound to arrive sooner or later. But I do hope they can come sooner, because I'm capable of better work and I don't want to have to wait until I'm an old man. Give me a chance to enjoy those freedoms now.

Such, then, are my demands, reflecting my own professional background. One thing I've learned from our helpful to-and-fro is that formulating a conceptual model of how things should *be* is not as pressing a matter as thinking about what we should *do*. It's said that you can only make one wish at a time, and I've already used up my quota. Other issues like equity, justice, law, and political reform are, of course, up for discussion too, and friends with backgrounds in those areas can focus on them, instead. Although it seems to me that freedom isn't necessarily most people's top priority, nobody wants to be in a constant state of fear and trepidation. It's my hope that we can create an even playing field that will make it possible for the poor to improve their lives, and that we can revitalize our culture so that the rich won't have to go on feeling inferior to foreigners, even when they have more money than them. And I hope that young people will be able to continue to discuss freely such topics as revolution, reform, and democracy, and can maintain their passionate commitment to the nation's future. Politics is not dirty, or pointless, or dangerous, or if it is, it's not true politics. Herbal medicines, gunpowder, silk, and pandas are not going to win us international glory, just as for the wife of a county chief to build up a collection of a hundred Louis Vuitton handbags is not going to win respect for our people. The party in power, I hope, can put its best foot forward and win itself some fame—in more than just the history books that you yourselves write.

247

This last year of mine

January 8, 2012

It's been several days since we saw the last of 2011. When I was in school, I hated having to write end-of-year reports, because — apart from the fact that I had nothing to report — I always felt there was no reason I should have to bare my soul to someone who forces you to perform a pre-appointed task, and I was sure I'd remember the things that deserved to be remembered. Later I discovered that memory isn't actually so reliable, so these days I'm willing to write things down.

Last year my performance in motor racing wasn't bad at all. Out of the eleven races in the national tournament, apart from the two occasions where my car broke down, I made it onto the prize-winners' podium on nine occasions and won the first championship for the Shanghai Volkswagen 333 team and turbo race. Last year I also won the first overall champion of the year title for the Subaru China rally team. The last time I won this title was in 2009. If you add in the championships I won in 2007 and 2008, I have won four first-place finishes overall. For that I want to thank my team colleagues and technicians. It was in 1993 that I saw the Hong Kong-

Beijing rally competition on TV for the first time, and that's when I got it into my head to race for the national team when I grew up. Sitting in front of the TV that day, I had a fantasy; now, eighteen years later, I have lived up to my aspirations as an eleven year old, and I'm very pleased. This doesn't mean that I'm urging everyone to always pursue their dream, because from 1993 to 2003 I completely forgot what I thought about that time in front of the TV. Only later, when circumstances allowed, did I consciously begin to practice driving. Maybe sometimes one clings stubbornly to something, and maybe sometimes one simply picks it up again when the moment is right—this can be true both of career goals and romantic attachments. Of course, this all depends on the individual and the situation—it's not a universal principle, but a matter of luck. I'm not proselytizing like someone you see hawking their books on the airport television.

In 2011 my friend Liu Caodong died. As the best rally driver in China he was my greatest rival. I managed to beat him in 2009, but lost to him in 2010. And in the blink of an eye, it's now been over three years since Xu Lang left us—in his time he was king of rally racing. I have a bone to pick with both of them, because their deaths have taken a lot of the excitement out of a victory. With them gone, even when I win it feels a bit of a shame, a bit like a monkey becoming king of the jungle because there are no more tigers. It's much the same story in the other things I do: In the absence of a hero, the stripling makes his name. Being both a monkey and a stripling, I seem to be a Gemini this coming year. I just wish I could have another race with Liu and Xu. Of course it makes no sense to say that—they're not going to come back to life, and I don't plan to die just yet. I say that simply to show how I cherish their memory.

Some leave us, and others join us. This last year I became a father. I love my daughter of course, but—more importantly—she loves me. As I expected, *Daddy* was her first word. A reporter asked me my preference: boy or girl. My answer was along these lines: I just hope that my daughter will be happy, and I am not concerned whether or not she is successful in the Chinese sense. Just so long as she has a good character I'm willing to create the best possible environment for her, sheltered from the pressures of this ruthless and unscrupulous society. Of course, she should do just what she wants to do, and she can try anything she fancies—all I am is a safety net when she takes a risk in climbing high. If in the future I suffer some setback that makes it difficult to support my daughter, then I've got no problem being a chauffeur for Robin Li, grinding ink for Bai Ye, or holding up a light for Chen Kaige.* Naturally I want to have a bigger family, and if I have a son then he's going to have to put up with things as they are, find a foothold in this reality, and pull out the stops to support himself and change society for the better.

2011 saw a big change in my own essays, but the shift actually began earlier. In my posts of 2009 and 2010 I would seize on the problems of the day and criticize the government, moved by a sense of disgust at things that were happening. Though I hate restrictions, I am also public-spirited enough to warn people about a hole in the road if I see one when I'm out driving at night. Every day I was looking forward to the time when China would suddenly turn into a society like the United States or Taiwan. I even felt that Hong Kong or Singapore are both imperfect, that the system is the root of all evil, that the system inevitably generates enormous abuses. For these criticisms I earned a lot of compliments, and I began to revel in all this appreciation and even subconsciously tried to cater to it. By 2010, many of my critiques hinged on assumptions of guilt and represented only variations on the same theme: The system is bad, the government is corrupt, tragedies are happening, and the people need help. In any society, I think, this kind of criticism is bound to be welcomed by readers at large: If the rulers are greedy and corrupt, there is bound to be serious antagonism between officials

251

* Robin Li is the CEO of Baidu, China's biggest Internet search engine; Bai Ye is a prominent Chinese literary critic; Chen Kaige is a well-known Chinese film director. At various times, Han Han has been critical of all three.

and the population. Anywhere you go, people like it when you say: "We're really in bad shape here! Your boss is a complete jerk—he's made a mess of so many things, but still he gets driven around in a smart car and has a mistress on the side. With all your talents, you deserve a lot more than you have—and what qualifies that asshole to be your boss, anyway? Everyone has the right to be boss or to change the boss, and the things he's got should be yours." With the exception of the boss, who won't be pleased to hear this, everyone else will feel you've expressed their thoughts exactly. If I write that kind of essay, and throw in a few little jokes for good measure, everyone's bound to agree that I've put things very well, and those who disagree with me will be written off as Fifty-centers, as the running dogs of the powerful, as enemies of the people. Even if someone wants to criticize me, they will first have to write a couple of pages that sing my praises before they can raise a couple of mild objections, otherwise they will easily provoke dissatisfaction and get branded with one negative label or another, in much the same way as the targets of my criticism like to pin labels on their opponents, with no room for consultation and compromise. When I discovered that people critical of me were getting fewer and fewer (or were becoming more and more cautious), I naturally was happy for a while, but later I came to feel uncomfortable with the whole scene, for I knew that no matter how right I was, I had to be wrong somewhere.

So, with time, I gradually reached the conclusion that a good writer shouldn't just train his sights on the high and mighty, he should also be ready to clip the wings of the masses. I began to make some changes early in 2011, with essays like the one about Village Chief Qian Yunhui, "Do we need the truth, or just the truth that fits our needs?" Of course, if both the mighty and the weak come in for criticism, I'll give priority to criticizing the former, for the simple reason that they're the ones who've got it easy, and ordinary citizens have got the raw end of the deal. But that's not to say that a good writer should suck up to the common people unconditionally, without a bottom line. If you say the people are so good and so right, so warm-hearted and so civilized, that they should have this and that and enjoy such-and-such and so-and-so, that the people have all kinds of God-given rights, that the people's eyes are not only gleaming with intelligence but are perfectly proportioned, as well . . . these phrases actually are no different for the kinds of insane flattery that Mao Zedong heaped on the masses before he took control, when they were just gambling chips in his effort to achieve power and prestige.

Some years ago, I was a committed revolutionary, believing that all one-party dictatorships had to be overthrown, that there had to be a multiparty democracy, direct elections, a tripartite division of power, and a nationalization of the armed forces. Friends would take issue with me then, arguing that a lot of people would get killed, that there'd be chaos, and that things would only get worse. My view at the time was: "Not necessarily—if we don't try it, how will we ever know? What you're telling me is just the ruling class's rationale for doing nothing, and besides, there's a price to pay whatever you do—if you don't take more extreme, more radical action, how are you going to eradicate the disease? It takes a big upheaval to create the conditions for excellent government. Besides, if the country ends up in chaos, it might give me the chance to be a warlord."

But gradually I have realized that this attitude doesn't differ very much in its emotional tenor from a dictator's offhand attitude: "Once I'm dead, the whole roof can come down, as far as I'm concerned." Extreme idealists who have lost connection with reality aren't necessarily the temperamental opposites of those who in reality are extreme authoritarians, and they may actually be sentimental bedfellows, although the banners they brandish may say completely different things. There's a good chance you'll end up as precisely the kind of person you once detested.

Therefore, I have no aspirations in other directions, but I will continue to keep demanding all the constitutionally permitted freedoms that have a bearing on my work—whether I'm sitting or standing, walking or writing or talking, I'll keep on demanding freedom until you can't stand it. We need to keep pushing; otherwise there will be no change. As for my writing, I hope in the New Year to be able to write things for my own pleasure, and I don't plan to suck up to anybody except my daughter. I'll write when I want, and leave ellipses when I don't.

Index

Environmental degradation, 209,
210
see also Pollution
Essays, student, 23–26
European Union, 76

F

Factory workers, quality of life of,
169–73
Feng Shunqiao, 79–80
Farmland, *see* Land
Fatherhood, 250–51
Federation of Literary and Art
Circles, 246
Ferrari, 76
Fifty-centers, 123, 129–31, 252
Flags at half-mast, 21–22, 39
Floods, 211
Foreign Affairs, Ministry of, 182
Foreign reporters, interviews with,
161–64
Founding of a Republic, The
(movie), 105–6, 216n
Foxconn, 171–73
France
boycotting businesses and
products from, 33–36, 38–40,
42, 73–77
defection of Chinese officials to,
76
demonstrations for Tibetan
independence in, 33, 43
incursion by forces from England
and, 44
restrictions on immigration from
China to, 36
Freedom [more]
pressing for, 245–47

Fujian Province, 145, 165, 167,
183

G

Gansu Province, 125–27
Fifty-centers in, 130
Gasoline, price of, 197–202
General Administration of Press
and Publication, 17
Generations, 1–3
Genetically engineered foods,
155
Global Times, 96, 204
Google, 122–23, 162, 224,
237n
Gorbachev, Mikhail, 246
Government officials, 125, 133–35,
141–42
bringing grievances to,
192
corrupt, *see* Corruption
defection to France of, 76
in Imperial China, 141
jail terms for "slandering" of,
145–49
mannerisms of, 205
public opinion poll on
performance of, 137–40
Graft, 80
see also Corruption
Great Relocation, The (Xie
Chaoping), 187n
Gross domestic product (GDP), 138,
140, 170, 173
per capita, 162, 163
Gu Changwei, 105
Guinness Book of World Records,
29

About the Author

Han Han was born in 1982 to middle-class parents. After dropping out of high school due to low grades, he wrote a novel, *Triple Door*, which became a runaway bestseller with more than twenty million copies in print. He has since become a star of the rally racing circuit and an international celebrity. He lives in Shanghai.